PAPERBACK SONGS

784.52
COU
PB

COUNTRY HITS

WITHDRAWN

W9-AJQ-154

EAU CLAIRE DISTRICT LIBRARY

MELODY LINE, CHORDS AND LYRICS
FOR KEYBOARD • GUITAR • VOCAL

HA

T 110556

BAT 5-2-97 $5.95

0-7935-5258-3

Copyright © 1995 by HAL LEONARD CORPORATION
International Copyright Secured All Rights Reserved

For all works contained herein:
Unauthorized copying, arranging, adapting, recording or public performance is an infringement of copyright.
Infringers are liable under the law.

This publication is not for sale in the E.C. and/or Australia or New Zealand.

7777 W. BLUEMOUND RD. P.O. BOX 13819 MILWAUKEE, WI 53213

Welcome to the PAPERBACK SONGS SERIES.

Do you play piano, guitar, electronic keyboard, sing or play any instrument for that matter? If so, this handy "pocket tune" book is for you.

The concise, one-line music notation consists of:

MELODY, LYRICS & CHORD SYMBOLS

Whether strumming the chords on guitar, "faking" an arrangement on piano/keyboard or singing the lyrics, these fake book style arrangements can be enjoyed at any experience level – hobbyist to professional.

The musical skills necessary to successfully use this book are minimal. If you play guitar and need some help with chords, a basic chord chart is included at the back of the book.

While playing and singing is the first thing that comes to mind when using this book, it can also serve as a compact, comprehensive reference guide.

However you choose to use this PAPERBACK SONGS SERIES book, by all means have fun!

CONTENTS

8 Achy Breaky Heart (Don't Tell My Heart)
Billy Ray Cyrus

11 Ain't Going Down ('Til the Sun Comes Up)
Garth Brooks

14 All the Gold in California
Gatlin Brothers

16 Always on My Mind
Willie Nelson

18 Angel of the Morning
Juice Newton

20 Any Day Now
Ronnie Milsap

22 Any Time
Eddy Arnold

24 Battle Hymn of Love
Kathy Mattea

28 Boot Scootin' Boogie
Brooks & Dunn

34 Bouquet of Roses
Eddy Arnold
Mickey Gilley

31 Brand New Man
Brooks & Dunn

36 Busted
John Conlee

38 By the Time I Get to Phoenix
Glen Campbell

37 Can't Help Falling in Love
Elvis Presley

40 The Chair
George Strait

43 Chattahoochee
Alan Jackson

46 Cold, Cold Heart
Hank Williams

48 Could I Have This Dance
Anne Murray

50 Crazy
Patsy Cline

52 Cryin' Time
Ray Charles

54 Daddy Sang Bass
Johnny Cash

56 Daddy's Hands
Holly Dunn

62 Down at the Twist and Shout
Mary Chapin Carpenter

66 Dream Baby (How Long Must I Dream)
Glen Campbell

59 Foolish Pride
Travis Tritt

68 For the Good Times
Ray Price

70 Forever and Ever, Amen
Randy Travis

74 Forty Hour Week
(For a Livin')
Alabama

80 Friends in Low Places
Garth Brooks

84 From Graceland to the
Promised Land
Merle Haggard

86 The Gambler
Kenny Rogers

88 Gentle on My Mind
Glen Campbell

77 God Bless the U.S.A.
Lee Greenwood

90 Goin' Through the Big D
Mark Chesnutt

96 Gone Country
Alan Jackson

93 Grandpa
(Tell Me 'Bout the Good Old Days)
The Judds

100 The Greatest Man I Never Knew
Reba McEntire

102 Green Green Grass of Home
Porter Wagoner

107 Hard Rock Bottom of
Your Heart
Randy Travis

110 He Stopped Loving Her Today
George Jones

112 The Heart Is a Lonely Hunter
Reba McEntire

104 Here You Come Again
Dolly Parton

116 Here's a Quarter
(Call Someone Who Cares)
Travis Tritt

122 Hey, Good Lookin'
Hank Williams

119 How Can I Help You
Say Goodbye
Patty Loveless

124 I Believe in You
Don Williams

130 I Can Love You Like That
John Michael Montgomery

136 I Fall to Pieces
Patsy Cline

127 I Feel Lucky
Mary Chapin Carpenter

138 I Just Fall in Love Again
Anne Murray

133 I Never Knew Love
Doug Stone

140 I Wouldn't Have Missed It
for the World
Ronnie Milsap

(contents continued)

142 I'll Still Be Loving You
Restless Heart

144 I'm Not Lisa
Jessi Colter

146 I've Come to Expect It From You
George Strait

152 I.O.U.
Lee Greenwood

154 It's a Heartache
Bonnie Tyler
Lorrie Morgan

156 It's Now or Never
John Schneider

158 Jambalaya (On the Bayou)
Hank Williams

160 The Keeper of the Stars
Tracy Byrd

162 Kentucky Rain
Elvis Presley

164 King of the Road
Roger Miller

166 Lay Down Sally
Eric Clapton

149 Lookin' for Love
Johnny Lee

168 Lost in the Fifties Tonight (In the Still of the Nite)
Ronnie Milsap

170 Love Without End, Amen
George Strait

174 Lucille
Kenny Rogers

179 Mammas Don't Let Your Babies Grow Up to Be Cowboys
Waylon Jennings & Willie Nelson

182 Neon Moon
Brooks & Dunn

190 No One Else on Earth
Wynonna Judd

192 Okie From Muskogee
Merle Haggard

194 On the Other Hand
Randy Travis

196 Pickup Man
Joe Diffie

200 A Rainy Night in Georgia
Brook Benton

202 Rocky Top
Lynn Anderson

204 Shameless
Garth Brooks

185 She Believes in Me
Kenny Rogers

208 She Is His Only Need
Wynonna Judd

214 She Thinks His Name Was John
Reba McEntire

216 Sixteen Tons
"Tennessee" Ernie Ford

218 Snowbird
Anne Murray

220 Somewhere in My Broken Heart
Billy Dean

222 Straight Tequila Night
John Anderson

224 To All the Girls I've Loved Before
Willie Nelson & Julio Iglesias

230 Tulsa Time
Don Williams

232 The Vows Go Unbroken (Always True to You)
Kenny Rogers

234 What's Forever For
Michael Martin Murphey

227 When She Cries
Restless Heart

240 Why Me? (Why Me, Lord?)
Kris Kristofferson

237 Wild One
Faith Hill

242 You Decorated My Life
Kenny Rogers

244 You Don't Know Me
Mickey Gilley

246 You Look So Good in Love
George Strait

248 You Needed Me
Anne Murray

250 Your Cheatin' Heart
Hank Williams

252 *Guitar Chord Guide*

ACHY BREAKY HEART
(Don't Tell My Heart)

Words and Music by
DON VON TRESS

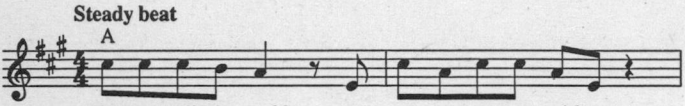

You can tell the world you nev - er was my girl.
You can tell your ma I moved to Ark - an - sas.

You can burn my clothes when I'm gone. Or
You can tell your dog to bite my leg. Or

you can tell your friends just what a fool I've been and
tell your broth-er Cliff whose fist can tell my lip. He

laugh and joke a - bout me on the phone.
nev - er real - ly liked me an - y - way. Or

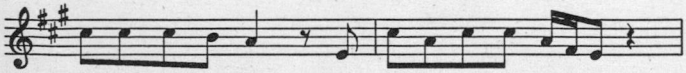

You can tell my arms go back to the farm.
tell your Aunt Lou-ise. Tell an - y - thing you please. My

Copyright © 1991 Millhouse Music
All Worldwide Rights Controlled by Songs Of PolyGram International, Inc.
International Copyright Secured All Rights Reserved

You can tell my feet to hit the floor. Or
self al - read - y knows I'm not o - kay. Or

you can tell my lips to tell my fin - ger - tips they
you can tell my eyes to watch out for my mind. It

won't be reach-ing out for you no more.
might be walk-ing out on me to - day. But

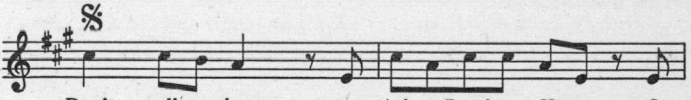

Don't tell my heart, my Ach - y Break-y Heart. I

just don't think he'd un - der - stand. And

if you tell my heart, my Ach - y Break-y Heart, he

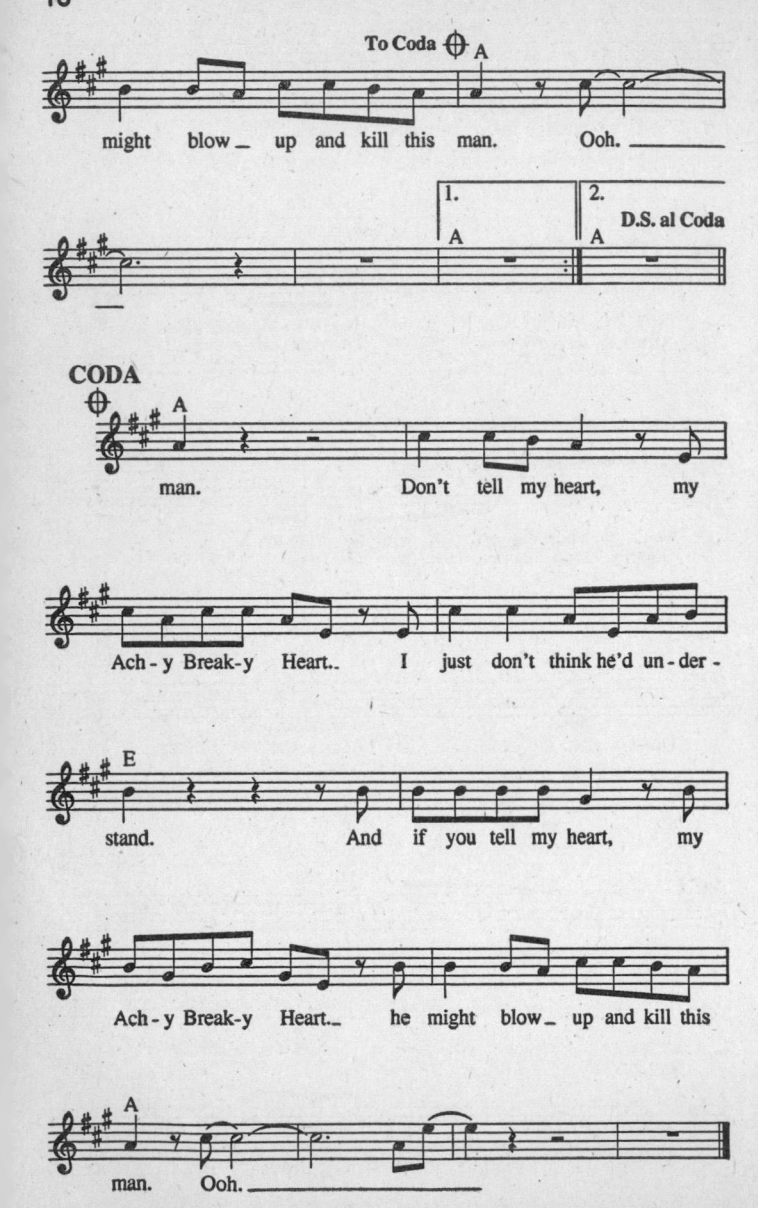
To Coda
A
might blow up and kill this man. Ooh.
1.
A
2.
A
D.S. al Coda
CODA
A
man. Don't tell my heart, my
Ach-y Break-y Heart. I just don't think he'd un-der-
E
stand. And if you tell my heart, my
Ach-y Break-y Heart. he might blow up and kill this
A
man. Ooh.

AIN'T GOING DOWN
('Til The Sun Comes Up)

Words and Music by KIM WILLIAMS,
GARTH BROOKS and KENT BLAZY

Bright Country

G

Six o' - clock on Fri - day eve - ning,
Nine o' - clock, the show is end - ing

Ma - ma does - n't know she's leav - ing
but the fun is just be - gin - ning.

'til she hears the screen door slam - ming,
She knows he's an - tic - i - pat - ing,

rub - ber squeal - ing, gears a - jam - ming,
but she's gon - na keep him wait - ing.

C

lo - cal Coun-try sta-tion just a blar-ing on the ra - di - o.
First, a bite to eat and then they're head-ing to the hon-ky- tonk, but

G

Pick him up at sev - en and they're
loud crowds and line danc - ing

D

head-ing to the ro - de - o. Ma-ma's on the front porch,
just ain't what they real - ly want. Drive out to the boon - docks

Copyright © 1993 Sony Cross Keys Publishing Co., Inc., Major Bob Music Co., Inc.,
No Fences Music, Inc. and Careers-BMG Music Publishing, Inc.
All Rights on behalf of Sony Cross Keys Publishing Co., Inc. Administered by Sony Music Publishing,
8 Music Square West, Nashville, TN 37203
International Copyright Secured All Rights Reserved

G
scream-ing out a warn-ing: "Girl, you'd bet-ter get your red head
and park down by the creek, where it's George Strait 'til real late and
1.
back in bed be-fore the morn-ing."
danc-ing cheek to cheek.
2.
C
They Ain't Go-ing Down 'til the
G
sun comes up, ain't giv-ing in 'til they
B♭ C
get e-nough. Go-ing 'round the world in a
pick-up truck.
G N.C. To Coda F G
Ain't Go-ing Down 'til the sun comes up.
F G
Ten 'til twelve is wine and danc-ing.
Six o'-clock on Sat-ur-day, her
Mid-night starts the hard ro-manc-ing.
folks don't know he's on his way. The

EAU CLAIRE DISTRICT LIBRARY

ALL THE GOLD IN CALIFORNIA

Words and Music by
LARRY GATLIN

© 1979 TEMI COMBINE INC. and SONGS OF ALL NATIONS
All Rights for TEMI COMBINE INC. Controlled by COMBINE MUSIC CORP.
and Administered by EMI BLACKWOOD MUSIC INC.
All Rights Reserved International Copyright Secured Used by Permission

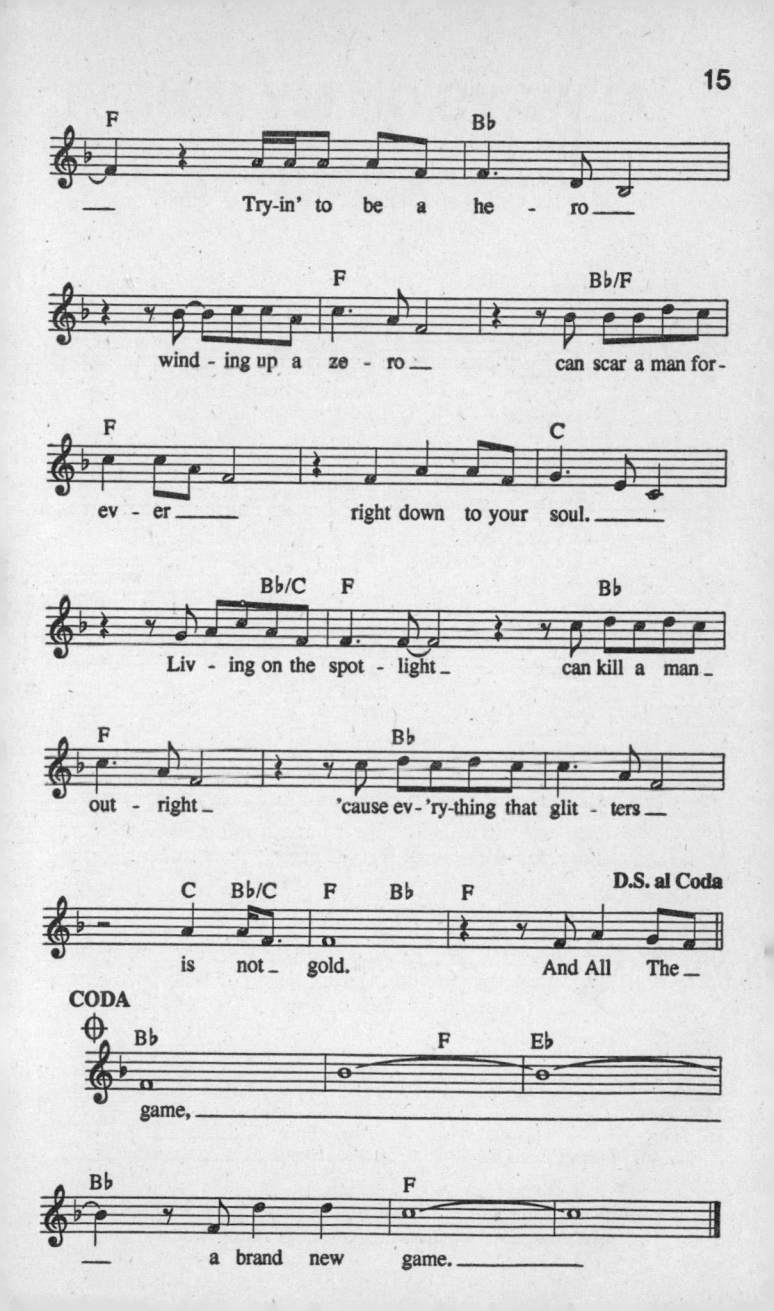
F
Bb
Try-in' to be a he - ro
F
Bb/F
wind - ing up a ze - ro
can scar a man for-
F
C
ev - er
right down to your soul.
Bb/C
F
Bb
Liv - ing on the spot - light
can kill a man
F
Bb
out - right
'cause ev-'ry-thing that glit - ters
C
Bb/C
F
Bb
F
D.S. al Coda
is not gold.
And All The
CODA
Bb
F
Eb
game,
Bb
F
a brand new game.

ALWAYS ON MY MIND

Words and Music by WAYNE THOMPSON,
MARK JAMES and JOHNNY CHRISTOPHER

Copyright © 1971, 1979 SCREEN GEMS-EMI MUSIC INC. and BUDDE SONGS INC.
All Rights Controlled and Administered by SCREEN GEMS-EMI MUSIC INC.
All Rights Reserved International Copyright Secured Used by Permission

D G/D D7 G D/A G7/B
You were Al-ways On My Mind; (You were Al-ways On My
1. 2.
C D7 To Coda G C D G C D
Mind.) you were Al-ways On My Mind. Mind.
G D/F# Em G/D C G/B
Tell me, tell me that your sweet love has-n't
Am Am7/D G D/F#
died, Give
Em G/D C G/B
me, give me one more chance to keep you sat - is -
Am D7 G D.S. al Coda
fied, sat - is - fied.
CODA
G D/F# Em G/D C G/D
Mind;
Am D7 G
you were Al-ways On My Mind.

ANGEL OF THE MORNING

Words and Music by
CHIP TAYLOR

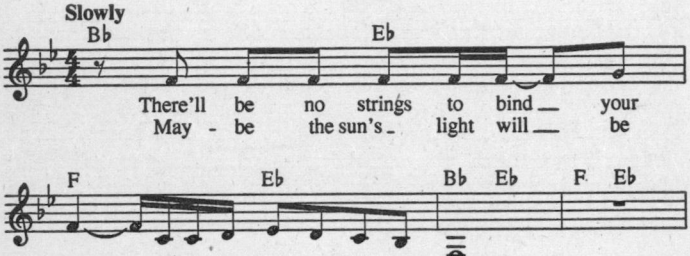

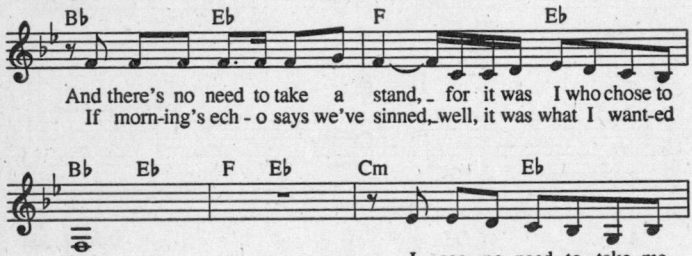

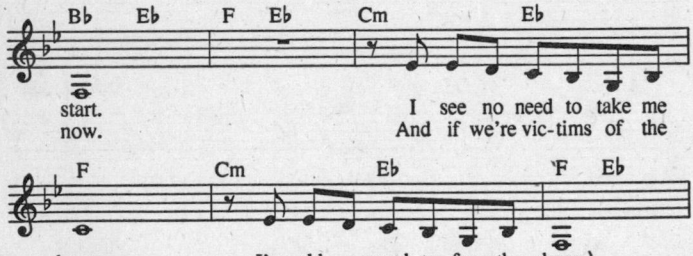

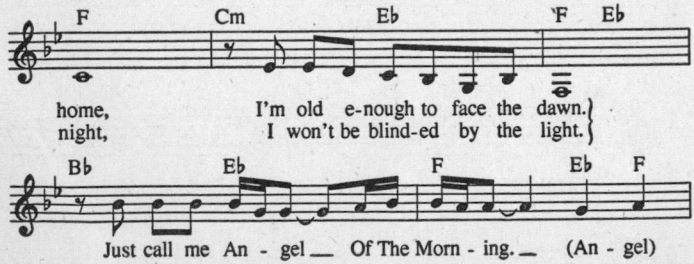

© 1967 EMI BLACKWOOD MUSIC INC.
All Rights Reserved International Copyright Secured Used by Permission

Bb Eb F Eb F
Just touch my cheek be - fore you leave me, ba - by.
Bb Eb F Eb F
Just call me An - gel Of The Morn - ing. (An - gel)
1. Eb Bb Eb F Eb
Then slow - ly turn a - way from me.
2. Eb
Then slow - ly turn a - way, I won't beg you to stay with
Bb Eb
me. Through the tears
Bb
of the day, of the
Eb F 3 F7
years. Ba - by, ba - by, ba - by,
Bb Eb F Eb F
Just call me An - gel Of The Morn - ing, (An - gel.)
Repeat and Fade
Bb Eb F Eb F
Just touch my cheek be - fore you leave me, ba - by.

ANY DAY NOW

Words and Music by BOB HILLIARD
and BURT BACHARACH

Copyright © 1962 by Unichappell Music Inc.
Copyright Renewed
International Copyright Secured All Rights Reserved

Am
B♭maj7
C7sus
F
don't _ want to stay. _ And yet un-til you're gone for-

Am
Dm
Am
ev-er _ I'll be hold - ing on _ for dear

Dm
C7sus
B♭
life, hold-ing you this way, _

C7sus
F
3
_ beg-gin' you to stay. An-y Day Now

Am
B♭maj7
when the clock strikes go, you'll call it off,

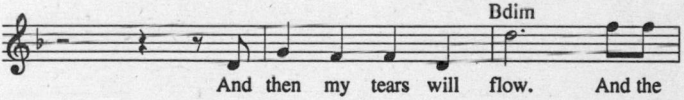
Bdim
And then my tears will flow. And the

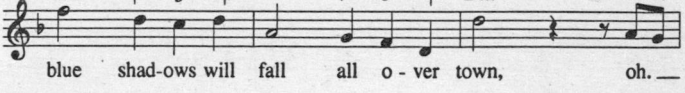
F
3
3
Dm
3
blue shad-ows will fall all o-ver town, oh. _

B♭m
F
_ An-y Day Now love will let me

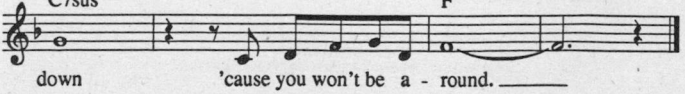
C7sus
F
down 'cause you won't be a-round. _

ANY TIME

Words and Music by
HERBERT HAPPY LAWSON

Copyright © 1921 by Unichappell Music Inc.
Copyright Renewed
International Copyright Secured All Rights Reserved

A7
you're think - ing 'bout me, That's the
D7
Db7 C7
3
time I'll be think - ing of
B7
you. So An - y
E7
Time you say you
A7
C#dim
want me back a - gain, That's the
D7
time I'll come back home to
G C
1.
G
2.
G
you. An - y

BATTLE HYMN OF LOVE

Words and Music by DON SCHLITZ
and PAUL OVERSTREET

© Copyright 1987 by MCA MUSIC PUBLISHING, A Division of MCA INC.,
DON SCHLITZ MUSIC, SCREEN GEMS-EMI MUSIC INC. and SCARLET MOON MUSIC
All Rights for DON SCHLITZ MUSIC Controlled and Administered by MCA MUSIC PUBLISHING,
A Division of MCA INC.
International Copyright Secured All Rights Reserved

MCA music publishing

To Coda
E
A
oth - er to take." (Female:)For rich or for poor,
D
un - der skies gray or blue, (Both:)till my
A
E
A
death I will stand by you.
(Male:) There are
wars and there are ru - mors. Wars yet to come.
E
Temp - ta - tions we'll have to walk
A
through. Though oth - ers may
D
trem - ble, I will not run. Till my

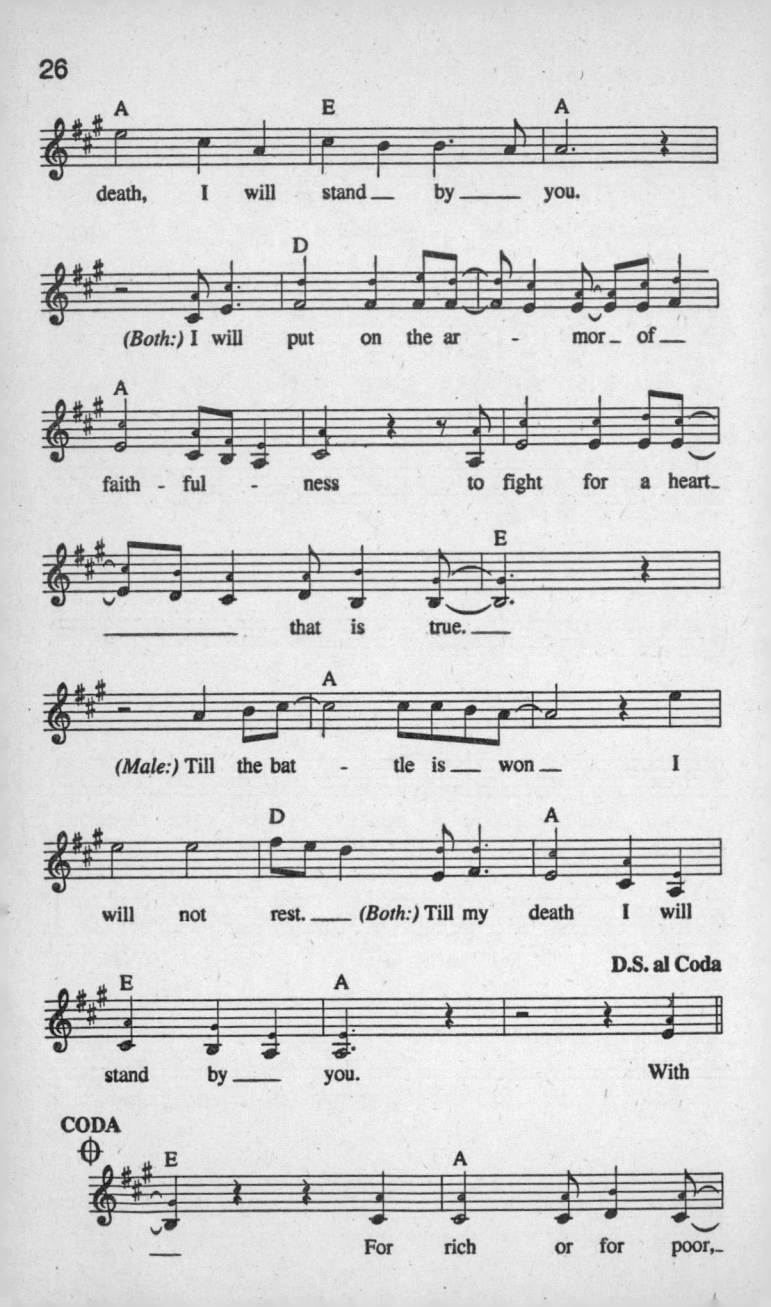
A E A
death, I will stand by you.
D
(Both:) I will put on the ar - mor of
A
faith - ful - ness to fight for a heart
E
that is true.
A
(Male:) Till the bat - tle is won I
D A
will not rest. (Both:) Till my death I will
D.S. al Coda
E A
stand by you. With
CODA
E A
For rich or for poor,

un - der skies gray or blue
D
A
till my death I will
E
A
stand by you. Till the bat -
- tle is won I will not
D
A
E
run. Till my death I will stand by
A
D
A
you.
(Instrumental)
D
A
E7
A

BOOT SCOOTIN' BOOGIE

Words and Music by
RONNIE DUNN

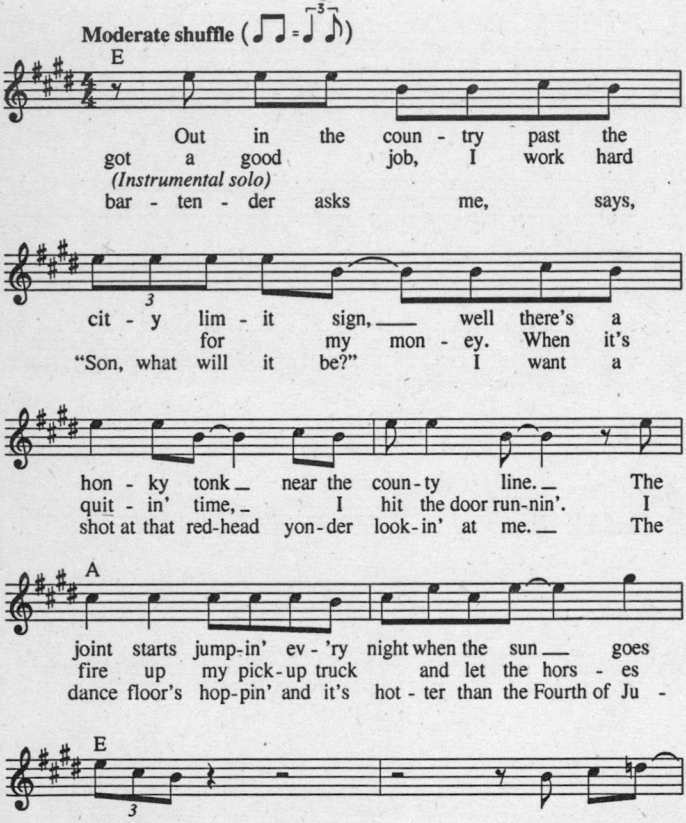

Copyright © 1991 Sony Tree Publishing Co., Inc. and Alfred Avenue Music
All Rights on behalf of Sony Tree Publishing Co., Inc. Administered by Sony Music Publishing,
8 Music Square West, Nashville, TN 37203
International Copyright Secured All Rights Reserved

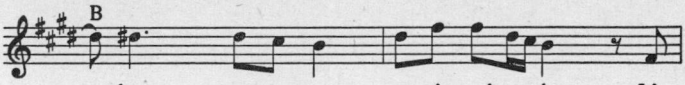

- key, wom-en, mu-sic and smoke. It's
in' down that high-way to that hide-a-way
- laws, in-laws, crooks and straights

where all the cow - boy folk go to Boot Scoot-in'
stuck out in the woods, to do the Boot Scoot-in'
all out mak-in' it shake do-in' the Boot Scoot-in'

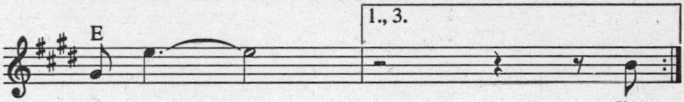

Boo - gic.
Boo - gie.
Boo - gie.

(Solo ends)

I've
The

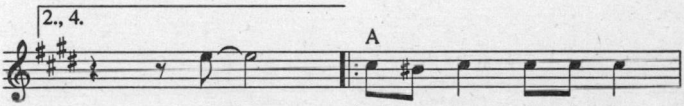

Yeah, heel to toe, do-cie doe,

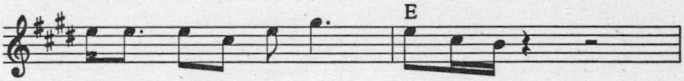

come on ba-by, let's go boot scoot-in'!

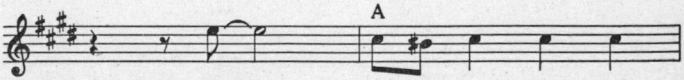

Woh, Cad-il-lac, Black-jack

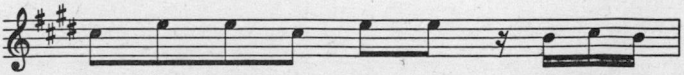

ba-by meet me out back, we're gon-na

E
boo-gie.
Oh, ___
B7
3
3
get down turn a - round, _ go to town, _ Boot Scoot-in'
E
1.
D.C.
Boo - gie. _____
2.
3.
Woh, _
I ____ said,
B7
3
3
get down, turn a - round, _ go to town, _ Boot Scoot-in'
E
Boo - gie. _____
Woh, _
B7
N.C.
3
3
get down, turn a - round, _ go to town, _ Boot Scoot-in'
E
A
E
Boo - gie. _____

BRAND NEW MAN

Words and Music by DON COOK,
RONNIE DUNN and KIX BROOKS

Copyright © 1991 Sony Tree Publishing Co., Inc., Showbilly Music,
Sony Cross Keys Publishing Co., Inc. and Fort Kix Music
All Rights Administered by Sony Music Publishing, 8 Music Square West, Nashville, TN 37203
International Copyright Secured All Rights Reserved

G
C/G
I was a roll - ing stone. I
now my heart beats true. Ba-by,
G
C
used to have a wild side, they say a coun-try mile wide. I'd
you and me to-geth-er feels more like for-ev-er than
(Instrumental solo on D.S.)
G
burn those beer joints down. That's all changed
an-y-thing I've ev - er known. We're right on track,
D
G
now, you turned my life a - round.
I ain't a-look-in' back.
C
Oh, I saw the light, I've been
D
G
bap - tised by the fire in your touch and the flame
C
D
in your eyes. I'm born to love a - gain,
1.
To Coda
G
C/G
I'm a Brand New Man.

G
C/G
2.
C/G
D.S. al Coda
I used to
CODA
C
Yeah, I saw the light, I've been
D
G
bap - tised by the fire in your touch and the flame
C
D
in your eyes. I'm born to love a - gain,
G
I'm a Brand New Man.
C
D
Yeah, I'm born to love a - gain,
I'm a Brand New
G
Man.

BOUQUET OF ROSES

Words and Music by STEVE NELSON
and BOB HILLIARD

Copyright © 1948 by Chappell & Co. and Better Half Music for the U.S.A. only
Copyright Renewed
All Rights outside the U.S.A. Administered by Chappell & Co.
International Copyright Secured All Rights Reserved

F
begged you to be dif - f'rent but you'll
know that I should hate you af - ter
C Ebdim C D7
al - ways be un - true, I'm tir - ed of for -
all you've put me thru; But how can I be
G7
giv - ing, Now there's noth - ing left to
bit - ter, When I'm still in love with
C G7
do.
you?
So I'm send - ing you a big Bou - quet Of
C G7
Ros - es, One for ev - 'ry
1.
C F
time you broke my heart.
C
2.
C F C
You heart.

BUSTED

Words and Music by HARLAND HOWARD

Copyright © 1962 Tree Publishing Co., Inc.
Copyright Renewed
All Rights Administered by Sony Music Publishing, 8 Music Square West, Nashville, TN 37203
International Copyright Secured All Rights Reserved

CAN'T HELP FALLING IN LOVE

Words and Music by GEORGE DAVID WEISS, HUGO PERETTI and LUIGI CREATORE

Copyright © 1961 by Gladys Music, Inc.
Copyright Renewed and Assigned to Gladys Music (Administered by Williamson Music)
International Copyright Secured All Rights Reserved

BY THE TIME I GET TO PHOENIX

Words and Music by
JIMMY WEBB

Copyright © 1967 by THE EMP COMPANY, New York, NY
International Copyright Secured All Rights Reserved

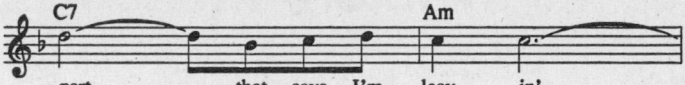
C7
Am
part that says I'm leav - in',
phone keep on ring - in',
think I'd real - ly leave her

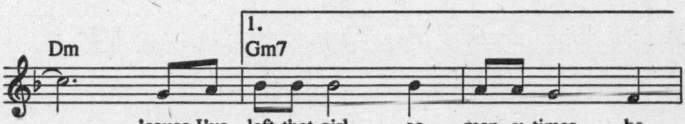
Dm
1.
Gm7
'cause I've left that girl so man - y times be -
off the
tho

E♭
C7
2.
Gm7
fore. By the wall,

E♭
C7
that's all. By the

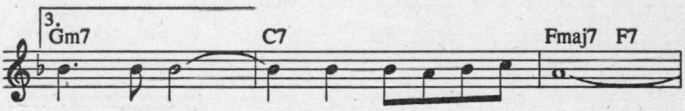
3.
Gm7
C7
Fmaj7 F7
time and time I've tried to tell her so,

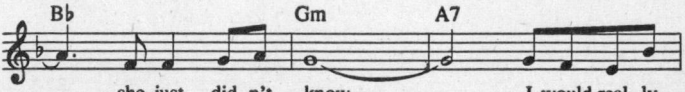
B♭
Gm
A7
she just did - n't know I would real - ly

D
go.

THE CHAIR

Words and Music by HANK COCHRAN
and DEAN DILLON

Copyright © 1985 Tree Publishing Co., Inc. and Nocturnal Eclipse Music
All Rights on behalf of Tree Publishing Co., Inc. Administered by Sony Music Publishing,
8 Music Square West, Nashville, TN 37203
All Rights on behalf of Nocturnal Eclipse Music Administered by Careers-BMG Music Publishing, Inc.
International Copyright Secured All Rights Reserved

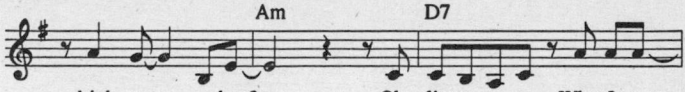

drink you a buy? Oh, lis-ten to me. What I mean

is can I buy you a drink? An- y -

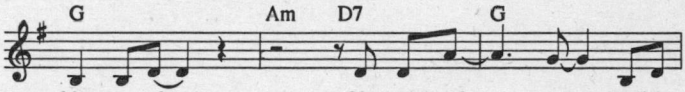

thing you please. Oh, you're wel - come. Well, I

don't think I caught your name. Are you wait-

- ing for some - one to meet you here? Well that makes

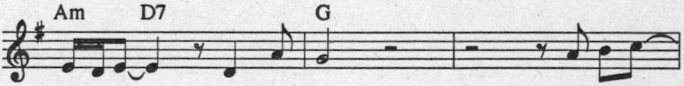

two of us; glad you came. No, I don't

know the name of the band, but they're good aren't

they? Would you care to dance? Yeah, I like

Am7 C/D
the song too, it re - minds me of you and me, ba -
G
- by, Do you think there's a chance that
Am D7
lat - er on I could drive you home? No,
G G/F# Em
I don't mind at all. Oh,
C Bm Am E7/G#
I like you too, and to tell you the truth that
Am D7 G Am/G G
was-n't my chair af - ter all. Oh,
C Bm Am E7/G#
I like you too, and to tell you the truth that
Am D7 G Am/G G
was-n't my chair af - ter all.

CHATTAHOOCHEE

Words and Music by JIM McBRIDE
and ALAN JACKSON

Bright Country 2-step

C

Way down yon-der on the Chat - ta - hoo - chee
fogged up the win-dows in ___ my old Chev - y;

G C

it gets hot - ter than a hoo - chie coo - chie,
I was will - in' but ___ she was-n't read-y. So, I

We laid rub - ber on the Geor - gia as - phalt.
set-tled for a bur - ger and a grape sno - cone. ___ I

G C

Got a lit - tle cra - zy but we nev - er got caught.
dropped her off ___ ear - ly but I did - n't go home.

𝄋 F

1.,2. Down by the riv - er on a Fri - day night, -
(D.S. Instrumental)

C G C

pyr - a - mid of cans in the pale moon - light,

Copyright © 1992 Sony Cross Keys Publishing Co., Inc., Seventh Son Music and Mattie Ruth Musick
All Rights on behalf of Sony Cross Keys Publishing Co., Inc.
Administered by Sony Music Publishing, 8 Music Square West, Nashville, TN 37203
International Copyright Secured All Rights Reserved

F
talk - ing 'bout cars and dream - in' 'bout wom - en.
D7
G
Nev - er had a plan; just a liv - in' for the min - ute.
C
(Solo ends) Yeah, way down yon - der on the
Chat - ta - hoo - chee; nev - er knew how much that mud - dy wa - ter
G
C
meant to me. But I learned how to swim and I
To Coda
learned who I was; a lot a - bout liv - in' and a
1.
G
C
lit - tle 'bout love.
(Instrumental)
G
C

G
C
2.
D.S. al Coda
G
C
Well, we lit - tle 'bout love.
CODA
G
C
lit - tle 'bout love, a lot a - bout liv - in' and a
G
C
N.C.
lit - tle 'bout love. (Instrumental)
C
G
C
G
C

COLD, COLD HEART

Words and Music by
HANK WILLIAMS

Copyright © 1951 by Hiriam Music and Acuff-Rose Music, Inc. in the U.S.A.
Copyright Renewed
All Rights for Hiriam Music Administered by Rightsong Music Inc.
All Rights outside the U.S.A. Controlled by Acuff-Rose Music, Inc.
International Copyright Secured All Rights Reserved

oth - er love be - fore my time made
was a time when I be - lieved that
C7
your heart sad and blue And so my heart is
you be - longed to me But now I know your
pay - ing now for things I did - n't
heart is shack - led to a mem - o -
F
do In an - ger, un - kind words are said that
ry The more I learn to care for you the
F7
Bb
C7
make the tear - drops start Why can't I free your
more we drift a - part Why can't I free your
1.
doubt - ful mind and melt your Cold, Cold
doubt - ful mind and
F
2.
F
Heart? You'll melt your Cold, Cold Heart?

COULD I HAVE THIS DANCE

Words and Music by WAYLAND HOLYFIELD
and BOB HOUSE

Copyright © 1980 Sony Tree Publishing Co., Inc. and PolyGram International Publishing, Inc.
All Rights on behalf of Sony Tree Publishing Co., Inc. Administered by Sony Music Publishing,
8 Music Square West, Nashville, TN 37203
International Copyright Secured All Rights Reserved

D
E7
rest of my life? Would you be my
D
E7
part - ner ev' - ry night?
1.
A
A7
D
When we're to - geth - er, it feels so
Dm
A
To Coda
right. Could I Have This Dance for the
E7
1.
A
E11
rest of my life? I'll
2.
A
E7
D.S. al Coda
life? Could
CODA
E7
A
rest of my life?
Bm7
E7
A

CRAZY

Words and Music by
WILLIE NELSON

Copyright © 1961 Sony Tree Publishing Co., Inc.
Copyright Renewed
All Rights Administered by Sony Publishing, 8 Music Square West, Nashville, TN 37203
International Copyright Secured All Rights Reserved

Ab
Wor - ry, why do I let my - self
Eb
F7
wor - ry; Won - d'rin'
Bb7
Bb7#5
what in the world did I do.
Eb
C7
Cra - zy for think - ing that my love could
Fm
hold you, I'm
Ab
Gm
Fm
Cm
Cra - zy for try - in', Cra - zy for cry - in' and I'm
Fm7
Bb7
Eb
Cra - zy for lov - in' you.

CRYIN' TIME

Words and Music by
BUCK OWENS

Copyright © 1964 Sony Tree Publishing Co., Inc., Beachaven Music Corp. and Jarest Music Company
Copyright Renewed
All Rights on behalf of Sony Tree Publishing Co., Inc. Administered by Sony Music Publishing,
8 Music Square West, Nashville, TN 37203
International Copyright Secured All Rights Reserved

fond - er and the tears are on - ly rain to make love

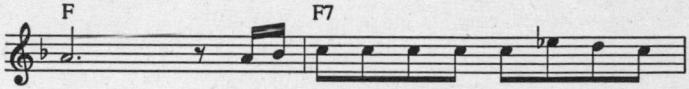

grow, well, my love for you could nev - er grow no

strong - er _____ if I live to be a hun - dred years

old. Oh, it's old. Oh, it's

Additional Lyrics

2. Now, you say that you've found someone you loved better;
That's the way it's happened every time before.
And as sure as the sun comes up tomorrow
Cryin' Time will start when you walk out the door.

(CHORUS)

DADDY SANG BASS

Words and Music by
CARL PERKINS

Copyright © 1968 Cedarwood Publishing and House of Cash, Inc.
All Rights for Cedarwood Publishing Administered by Songs Of PolyGram International, Inc.
International Copyright Secured All Rights Reserved

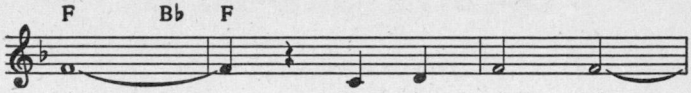
F Bb F
throne. No, the cir - cle

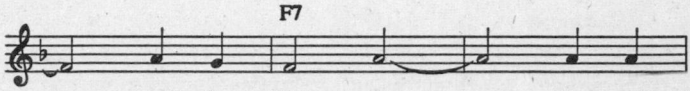
F7
won't be bro - ken, Bye and

Bb F C7
bye, Lord, bye and bye.

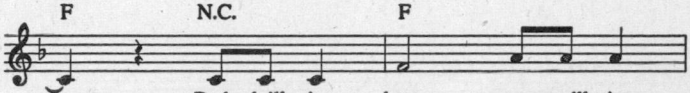
F N.C. F
Dad - dy'll sing bass, ma - ma'll sing

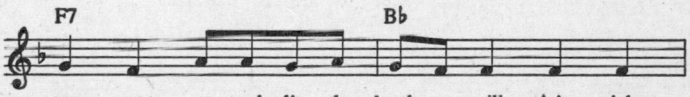
F7 Bb
ten - or, me and lit - tle broth - er will join right

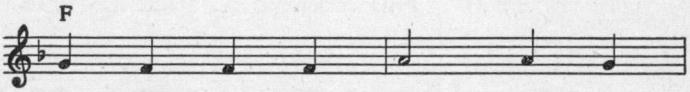
F
in there in the sky, Lord

Bb C7 F
in the sky.

DADDY'S HANDS

Words and Music by
HOLLY DUNN

© 1986 EMI BLACKWOOD MUSIC INC.
All Rights Reserved International Copyright Secured Used by Permission

D
1.
A
D
- ry had left their mark be - hind.
- ber the
- ed the
2., 3.
A
D
I re - love in Dad - dy's Hands.
love in Dad - dy's Hands.
Dad-dy's Hands were soft and
G
D
F♯m
kind when I was cry - ing. Dad-dy's Hands
Bm
G
A
were hard as steel when I'd done wrong.
D
Dad-dy's Hands weren't al - ways gen-tle but I've

G
E
come to un - der - stand, there was
To Coda
D
G
D/F#
A7/E
D
al - ways love in Dad-dy's Hands.
1.
G
D/F#
A/E
(Instrumental)
D
2.
D.S. al Coda
I re - Dad-dy's
CODA
D
Asus
love
A
D
G
in Dad-dy's Hands. (Instrumental)
D/F#
A/E
D

FOOLISH PRIDE

Words and Music by
TRAVIS TRITT

Copyright © 1994 Post Oak Publishing, Inc.
International Copyright Secured All Rights Reserved

Bb C F
it just shows weak - ness. So, the
he's lost his best friend and

Bb C Dm
hurt goes on with ev - 'ry tear she's cried.
more than just a lov - er can pro - vide.

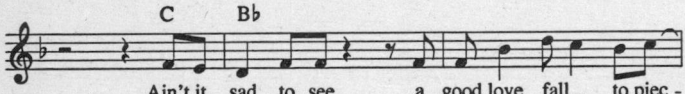
C Bb
Ain't it sad to see a good love fall to piec -
So, he wrest-les with e - mo-tions that de-feat

F Bb F
- es? Chalk an - oth - er heart break up
him. Chalk an - oth - er love lost up

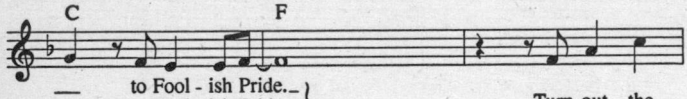
C F
to Fool - ish Pride.
to Fool - ish Pride.
Turn out the

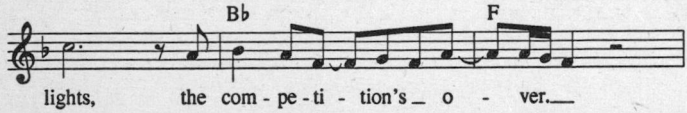
Bb F
lights, the com - pe - ti - tion's o - ver.

Bb Gm7
The stub-born souls are the los - ers here to-night.

C
F
And while the bridg - es burn
Bb
F
an - oth - er hard, hard les - son's learned
Bb
Gm7
as in the ash - es pas - sion slow - ly dies
C7
Dm
And this ro - mance goes down
1. Bb
C
F
Eb
to Fool - ish Pride,
yeah.
F
Eb
2. Bb
C
He
to Fool - ish Pride
Dm
C
Bb
Am
Gm7
Chalk an - oth - er love lost up
C
F
Eb
to Fool - ish Pride,
yeah.
F
Eb
F

DOWN AT THE TWIST AND SHOUT

Words and Music by
MARY CHAPIN CARPENTER

Fast Country two-beat

D

Sat-ur-day night and the moon is out. I wan-na

A

head on o-ver to the Twist and Shout, find a

E

two-step part-ner and a Ca-jun beat, when it

A

lifts me up, I'm gon-na find my feet

D E

out in the mid-dle of a big dance floor. When I

A

hear that fid-dle, wan-na beg for more. Wan-na

E A

dance to a band from a-Loui-si-an' to-night.

© 1990 EMI APRIL MUSIC INC. and GETAREALJOB MUSIC
All Rights Controlled and Administered by EMI APRIL MUSIC INC.
All Rights Reserved International Copyright Secured Used by Permission

E
And I nev - er have wan-dered down to
al - li - ga - tor stew and a
ma - ma, bring your pa - pa, bring your
A
New Or - leans, nev - er have drift - ed down a
craw - fish pie, a gulf storm blow - in' in - to
sis - ter too. They got lots of mu - sic and
E
bay - ou stream. But I heard that mu - sic on the
town to-night. Liv - in' on the del - ta it's quite
lots of room. When they play you a waltz from a
A
ra - di - o, and I swore some - day I was
a show. They got hur - ri-cane par-ties ev - 'ry
nine - teen - ten, you're gon-na feel a lit-tle bit
F#m
gon - na go: down a - High - way 10, past a -
time it blows. But here up north it's a
young a - gain. Well, you learn to dance with your
B7
La - fay-ette; there's a Bat - on Rouge. And I
cold, cold rain, and there ain't no cure for my
rock - in' roll, you learn to swing with

E
won't for-get to send you a card with
blues to-day; ex-cept when the pa-per says
do-si-do. But you learn to love at the
my re-grets 'cause I'm nev-er gon-na come back home.
Beou-so-leil is a com-in' in-to town. Ba-by,
fais do do when you hear a lit-tle Jolie Blon.
A
D
let's go down. It's Sat-ur-day night and the
A
moon is out. I wan-na head on o-ver to the
E
Twist and Shout, find a two-step part-ner and a
A
Ca-jun beat. When it lifts me up, I'm gon-na
D
find my feet out in the mid-dle of a
E
A
big dance floor. When I hear that fid-dle, wan-na

E
beg for more. Wan-na dance to a band from a -
A
Loui-si - an'___ to-night. Hey!
(Whoo!)
D
A
(Instrumental)
E
1.
2.
A
To Coda
D.S. al Coda
They got a
Bring your
CODA
D
E
A
E
A
D D7 D

DREAM BABY
(How Long Must I Dream)

Words and Music by
CINDY WALKER

© 1962 (Renewed 1990) TEMI COMBINE INC.
All Rights Controlled by COMBINE MUSIC CORP. and Administered by EMI BLACKWOOD MUSIC INC.
All Rights Reserved International Copyright Secured Used by Permission

me stop my dream - in' You can make my dreams come
D
A7
true Sweet Dream
Ba - by Sweet
Dream Ba - by
D7
Sweet Dream Ba - by
A7
How long must I
1.
D
dream?
2.
D
dream?

FOR THE GOOD TIMES

Words and Music by
KRIS KRISTOFFERSON

Copyright © 1968 by Careers–BMG Music Publishing, Inc.
International Copyright Secured All Rights Reserved

N.C.
F
Lay your head up-on my
C7
pil-low, Hold your warm and ten-der
F
bod-y close to mine. Hear the
Fmaj7
F6
F
whis-per of the rain-drops blow-ing
B♭
B♭/A
B♭6
soft a-gainst the win-dow
C7
Gm7
And make be-lieve you love me one more
C7
3
1.
F
F6
time For The Good Times.
F
F6
2.
F
I'll get a- Times.

FOREVER AND EVER, AMEN

Words and Music by DON SCHLITZ
and PAUL OVERSTREET

© Copyright 1987 by MCA MUSIC PUBLISHING, A Division of MCA INC.,
DON SCHLITZ MUSIC, SCREEN GEMS–EMI MUSIC INC. and SCARLET MOON MUSIC
All Rights for DON SCHLITZ MUSIC Controlled and Administered by MCA MUSIC PUBLISHING,
A Division of MCA INC.
International Copyright Secured All Rights Reserved
MCA music publishing

___ that I'm kill - in'. I'm
___ on a mem - 'ry, Make

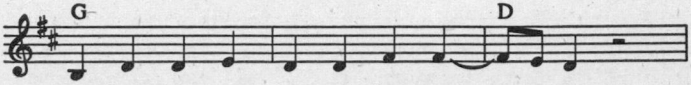

no long - er one___ of those guys.___
peo - ple for - get___ things they knew.___

As sure as I live___ this
Well it's eas - y to see___ it's

love that I give.___ is gon - na be yours.
hap-pen - in' to me.___ I've al - read - y for - got -

___ un - til the day that I___ die.___ Oh ba - by,
- ten ev - 'ry wom - an but___ you.___ Oh dar - lin'

I'm gon - na love___ you for ev - er,___

For - ev - er And Ev - er, A - men.___

G
As long as old men sit and
D
E7
talk a - bout the weath - er, as long as old wom -
A
- en sit and talk a - bout old men; if you
D
G
D
won - der how long I'll be faith - ful
G
I'll be hap - py to tell you a - gain.
well just lis - ten to how this song
E7
G
ends;
I'm gon - na love
A
D
G
you for - ev - er and ev - er, For -

E7
A7
D
ev - er And Ev - er, A - men.
1.
G
A
D
(Instrumental)
G
E
A
D
2.
G
They say I'm gon - na love
A
D
G
you for - ev - er and ev - er, for -
E7
A
Bm
ev - er and ev - er, for - ev - er and ev -
G
E7
Asus
- er, For - ev - er And Ev - er,
N.C.
D
A - men.

FORTY HOUR WEEK
(For A Livin')

Words and Music by DAVE LOGGINS,
DON SCHLITZ and LISA SILVER

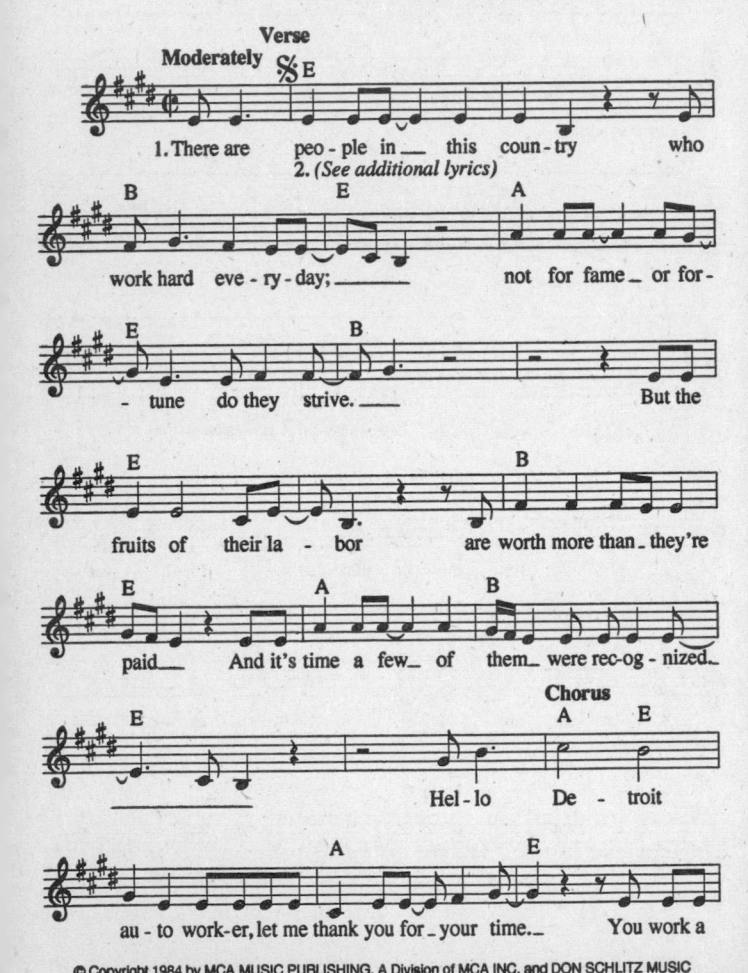

© Copyright 1984 by MCA MUSIC PUBLISHING, A Division of MCA INC. and DON SCHLITZ MUSIC
All Rights Controlled and Administered by MCA MUSIC PUBLISHING, A Division of MCA INC.
International Copyright Secured All Rights Reserved
MCA music publishing

A
E
For-ty Hour Week for a liv-in' just to
B
E
send it on down the line. Hel-lo
A
E
A
Pitts - burgh steel mill work-er, let me thank you for your time.
E
A
E
You work a For-ty Hour Week for a liv-in'
B
E
just to send it on down the line.
Bridge 1
B
This is for the one who swings the ham-mer,
A
E
B
driv - in' home the nail; for the one be-hind the
A
E
coun - ter ring - in' up the sales; for the
C#m
G#m
one who fights the fire, the one who brings the

Additional Lyrics

Verse 2:
You can see them every morning
In the factories and the fields,
In the city streets and the quiet country towns.
Workin' together like spokes inside a wheel,
They keep this country turnin' around.

Chorus 2:
Hello Kansas wheatfield farmer,
Let me thank you for your time.
You work a Forty Hour Week for a livin'
Just to send it on down the line.
Hello West Virginia coal miner,
Let me thank you for your time.
You work a Forty Hour Week for a livin'
Just to send it on down the line.

Bridge 2:
This is for the one who drives the big rig
Up and down the road;
For the one out in the warehouse
Bringin' in the load;
For the waitress, the mechanic,
The policeman on patrol;
For everyone who works behind the scenes...*(2nd ending)*

GOD BLESS THE U.S.A.

Words and Music by
LEE GREENWOOD

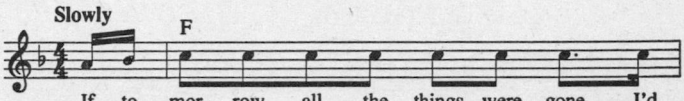

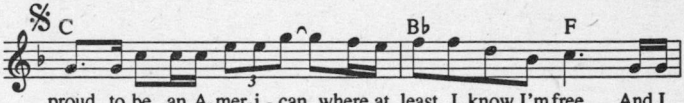

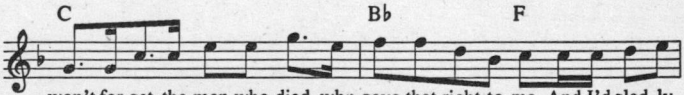

© Copyright 1984 by MUSIC CORPORATION OF AMERICA, INC. and SONGS OF POLYGRAM INTERNATIONAL, INC.
All Rights Controlled and Administered by MUSIC CORPORATION OF AMERICA, INC.
International Copyright Secured All Rights Reserved
MCA music publishing

Dm
Am7
Bb
Am7
stand up; next to you and de-fend her still to-day. 'Cause there
To Coda
Gm7
F
Bb
C11
ain't no doubt I love this land God Bless The U. S.
F
Fmaj9
Bb
F
A.
Bb
F
From the lakes of Min - ne - so - ta, to the
Bb
Gm7
hills of Ten-nes-see, a - cross the plains of Tex - as from
Eb7
C7
F
sea to shin - ing sea, From De-troit down to Hous-ton and
Am7
Gm7
New York to L. A. Well, there's pride in ev-'ry A-mer-i-can heart, and it's

Dm
Bb
D.S. al Coda
time to stand and say
That I'm
CODA
F
Bb
C11
Dm
God Bless The U. S. A.
Bb
C
And I'm proud to be an A-mer-i-can where at
Bb
F
C
least I know I'm free, and I won't for-get the men who died, who
Bb
F
Dm
Am7
gave that right to me. And I'd glad-ly stand up next to you, and de-
Bb
Am7
Gm7
F
fend her still to-day. 'Cause there ain't no doubt I love this land
Gm7
Am7
Bb
C7
F
God Bless The U. S. A.

FRIENDS IN LOW PLACES

Words and Music by DEWAYNE BLACKWELL
and EARL BUD LEE

Copyright © 1990 by Careers–BMG Music Publishing, Inc. and Music Ridge Music
International Copyright Secured All Rights Reserved

B♭dim7
Bm7
fear in his eyes when I took his glass of cham-pagne
cause a big scene just give me an ho - ur and
Bm7♭5/D
E
and I toast-ed you, said,"Hon-ey,
then, well I'll be as high as that i -
we may be through but you'll nev-er hear me com-plain."
- vo-ry tow - er that you're liv-in' in.
A
'Cause I've got Friends In
Low Plac - es where the whis-key drowns and the
Bm7
beer chas - es my blues a - way
E
and I'll be o - kay. Yeah,

A
I'm not big on so - cial grac - es. Think I'll
slip on down to the o - a - sis. Oh,
Bm7
E
A
To Coda
I've got Friends In Low Plac - es.
(Instrumental)
Bm7
E
A
D.S. al Coda
Well, I
CODA
I've got Friends In

Low Plac - es where the whis - key drowns and the
Bm7
beer chas - es my blues a - way
E
and I'll be o - kay.
A
Yeah, I'm not big on
so - cial grac - es. Think I'll slip on down to the
Bm7
o - a - sis. Oh, I've got Friends
E
A
Repeat and Fade
In Low Plac - es.

FROM GRACELAND TO THE PROMISED LAND

Words and Music by
MERLE HAGGARD

Copyright © 1977 Tree Publishing Co., Inc.
All Rights Administered by Sony Music Publishing, 8 Music Square West, Nashville, TN 37203
International Copyright Secured All Rights Reserved

A7
could-n't help but lis-ten when he
D
G
sang. It's a long way from
long way from
To Coda
Em/A
D
Mem-phis to that man-sion in the
Grace-land a-cross Jor-dan to the
D
A
sky, But he kept his faith in
D.S. al Coda
D D6 D7 D
Je-sus all a-long. It's a
CODA
G
D
Prom-ised Land, But Je-sus fi-n'lly
A A7 D
came to lead him home.

THE GAMBLER

Words and Music by
DON SCHLITZ

1. On a warm sum - mer's eve - ning on a
2. "Son I've made a life out of
3. - 5. *(See additional lyrics)*

train bound for no - where, I met up with a gam - bler. We were
read-in' peo-ple's fac - es and know-in' what their cards were by the

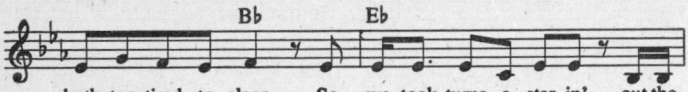

both too tired to sleep. So we took turns a - star - in' out the
way they held their eyes. So if you don't mind my say - in' I can

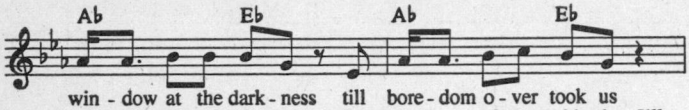

win - dow at the dark - ness till bore - dom o - ver took us
see you're out of ac - es; for a taste of your whis - key I'll

and he be-gan to speak. He said give you some ad-vice."

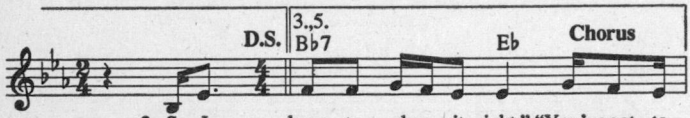

3. So I learn to play it right." "You've got to

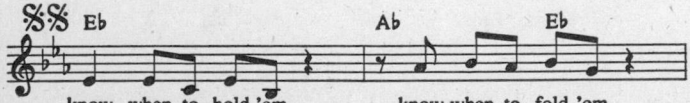

know when to hold 'em, know when to fold 'em.

Copyright © 1977 Sony Cross Keys Publishing Co., Inc.
All Rights Administered by Sony Music Publishing, 8 Music Square West, Nashville, TN 37203
International Copyright Secured All Rights Reserved

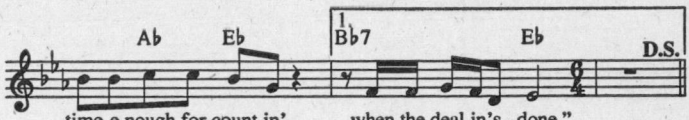

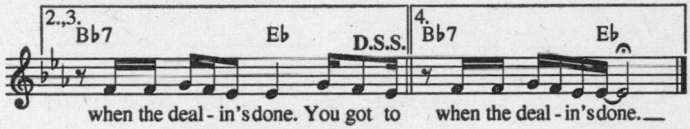

Additional Lyrics

3. (So I) handed him my bottle,
And he drank down my last swallow.
Then he bummed a cigarette and
Asked me for a light.
And the night got deathly quiet and
His face lost all expression.
Said, "If you're gonna play the game,
Boy, you gotta learn to play it right."
(CHORUS)

4. "Ev'ry gambler knows that the secret to survivin'
Is knowin' when to throw away, and
Knowin' what to keep.
'Cause ev'ry hand's a winner, and
Ev'ry hand's a loser.
And the best that you can hope for
Is to die in your sleep." And...

5. When he'd finished speakin'
He turned back toward the window.
Crushed out his cigarette and
Faded off to sleep.
And somewhere in the darkness
The Gambler he broke even.
But in his final words I found
An ace that I could keep.
(CHORUS)

GENTLE ON MY MIND

Words and Music by
JOHN HARTFORD

Copyright © 1967, 1968 by Ensign Music Corporation
International Copyright Secured All Rights Reserved

Additional Lyrics

2. It's not clinging to the rocks and ivy planted on their columns now that binds me
Or something that somebody said because they thought we fit together walkin'.
It's just knowing that the world will not be cursing or forgiving when I walk along
Some railroad track and find
That you're moving on the backroads by the rivers of my memory and for hours
You're just Gentle On My Mind.

3. Though the wheat fields and the clothes lines and junkyards and the highways
Come between us
And some other woman crying to her mother 'cause she turned and I was gone.
I still run in silence, tears of joy might stain my face and summer sun might
Burn me 'til I'm blind
But not to where I cannot see you walkin' on the backroads by the rivers flowing
Gentle On My Mind.

4. I dip my cup of soup back from the gurglin' cracklin' cauldron in some train yard
My beard a roughning coal pile and a dirty hat pulled low across my face.
Through cupped hands 'round a tin can I pretend I hold you to my breast and find
That you're waving from the backroads by the rivers of my memory ever smilin'
Ever Gentle On My Mind.

GOIN' THROUGH THE BIG D

Words and Music by MARK WRIGHT,
RONNIE ROGERS and JON WRIGHT

Moderate Country

A

Six short months we went to-geth - er, de-
Things like this are nev - er fi - nal.

E A

cid - ed it should be___ for-ev - er. Two pay - checks were
I'm still pay - ing on___ the vi - nyl floor-ing in the

D B

bet-ter than one. A dia-mond ring,_ it was done.
laun - dry room; it's mul - ti - col-ored, wa-ter-proof.

E A

Bought her a house like I
It's a lit - tle bit tough to___

E A

said I would_ in a sub - di - vid - ed neigh-bor - hood._ The
face my friends,_the_ ones that said that I jumped in___ the

D B

fuse got short and the nights got _ long. It was o-ver, long gone
riv - er of love a lit - tle too soon. That was Au - gust,

© 1994 EMI BLACKWOOD MUSIC INC., MAYPOP MUSIC (A Division of WILDCOUNTRY, INC.)
and SONGS OF JASPER, INC.
All Rights Reserved International Copyright Secured Used by Permission

E
be-fore I knew
and this is June,
where I was head-ed
and it's a dif-f'rent
A
to.
tune.
I'm Go- in' Through The Big D and
E
A
don't mean Dal-las. I can't be-lieve what the judge had to tell us.
D
I got the jeep and she got the pal - ace.
A
E
I'm Go-in' Through The Big D and don't mean
1.
A
E
Dal - las.
2.
A
E
Dal-las. (Instrumental)
A

D
A
E
A
I'm
E
Go- in' Through The Big D and don't mean Dal-las. I can't be-lieve what the
A
judge had to tell _ us. I got the jeep, she got the
two bed-room, mort - gage is due, sid - ing light-blue
D
A
E
pal - ace. I'm Go-in' Through The Big D and don't mean
A
N.C.
Dal - las. I'm Go-in' Through The Big D and
A
don't mean Dal - las. (Instrumental)
E
A

GRANDPA
(Tell Me 'Bout The Good Old Days)

Words and Music by
JAMIE O'HARA

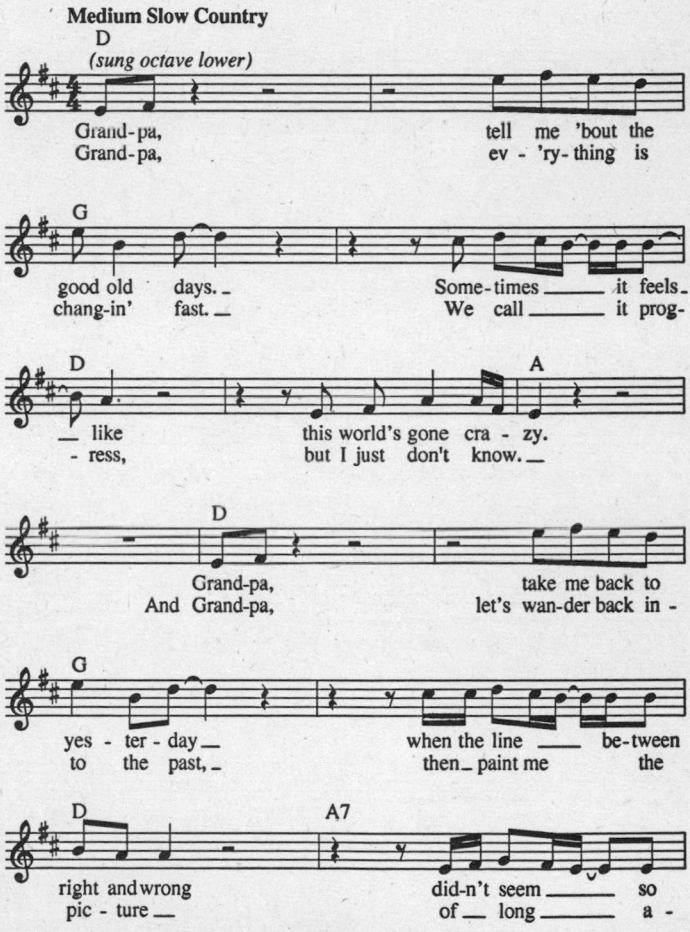

Copyright © 1985 Sony Cross Keys Publishing Co., Inc.
All Rights Administered by Sony Music Publishing, 8 Music Square West, Nashville, TN 37203
International Copyright Secured All Rights Reserved

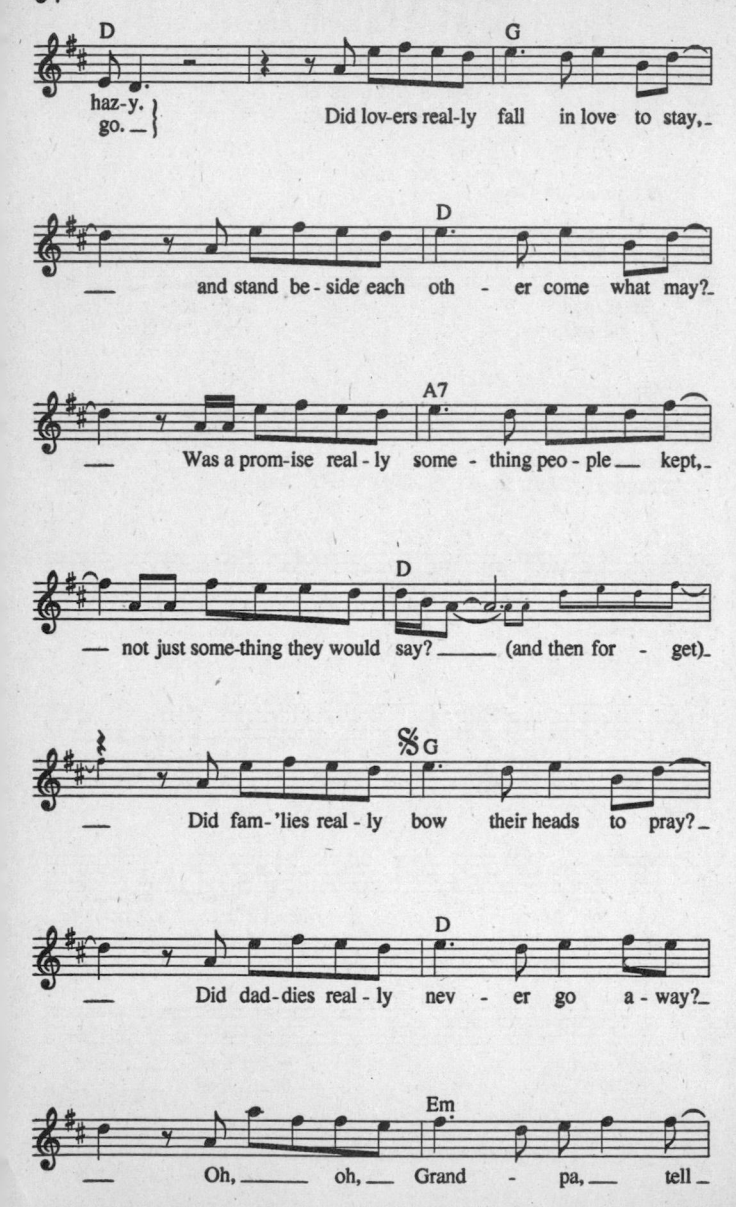
D
G
haz-y.
go. —
Did lov-ers real-ly fall in love to stay,
D
— and stand be-side each oth - er come what may?
A7
— Was a prom-ise real-ly some - thing peo-ple — kept,
D
— not just some-thing they would say? — (and then for - get)
𝄋G
— Did fam-'lies real-ly bow their heads to pray?
D
— Did dad-dies real-ly nev - er go a-way?
Em
— Oh, — oh, — Grand - pa, — tell

G/A
1.
D
me 'bout the good old days.
2.
D
Em
Oh, oh, Grand - pa, tell
G/A
D
me 'bout the good old days.
G
(Instrumental)
D
A7
D
D.S. and Fade
Did fam-'lies real - ly

GONE COUNTRY

Words and Music by
BOB McDILL

Copyright © 1994 PolyGram International Publishing, Inc. and Ranger Bob Music
International Copyright Secured All Rights Reserved

C D G
ror, and she on - ly ag - es.
out a - gainst wealth and priv - ilege.
scene just ain't gon - na ral - ly.
D C G
She's been read - in' 'bout Nash-ville and all the
He says, "I don't be-lieve in mon-ey, but a
He says, "Hon - ey, I'm a se - ri - ous com-pos -
C D G
rec - ords that ev - 'ry- bod - y's buy - ing.
man could make him a kill - in',
er, schooled in voice and com - po - si - tion,
D C G
Says, "I'm a sim - ple girl my - self;
'cause some of that stuff don't
but with the crime and the smog these days
C D G
grew up on Long Is - land."
sound much dif - f'rent than Dyl - an.
L. A.'s no place for chil - dren.
D C Em
So, she packs her bags to
I hear down there it's
Lord, it sounds so eas - y. It

D
Em
try her hand. Says, "This might be
changed, you see. They're not as back-ward as they
should - n't take long. Be back in the mon - ey in
D
G
my last chance." She's Gone Coun - try.
used to be." He's Gone Coun - try.
no time at all." He's Gone Coun - try.
C
D
G
Look at them boots. She's Gone Coun - try,
Look at them boots. He's Gone Coun - try,
Look at them boots. He's Gone Coun - try,
C
D
G
back to her roots. She's Gone Coun-try, a
back to his roots. He's Gone Coun-try, a
back to his roots. He's Gone Coun-try, a
C
D
Em
To Coda
new kind of suit. She's Gone Coun - try.
new kind of suit. He's Gone Coun - try.
new kind of suit. He's Gone Coun - try.
1.
G
D
C
(Spoken:) Here she comes!
(Instrumental)

G
D
C
2.
Well, the
(Spoken:) Here he comes!
(Instrumental)
G
C
D
G
C
D
G
C
D
Em
D.S. al Coda
He com -
CODA
G
D
C
(Spoken:) Here he comes!
(Instrumental)
G
D
C
Yeah, he's Gone
G
C
D
Coun - try,
a new kind of walk.
gonna make his move.
He's Gone
Repeat ad lib. and Fade
G
C
D
Coun - try,
a new kind of talk.
back to his roots.
He's Gone

THE GREATEST MAN I NEVER KNEW

Words and Music by RICHARD LEIGH
and LAYNG MARTINE, JR.

© 1991 EMI APRIL MUSIC INC., LION-HEARTED MUSIC and LAYNG MARTINE JR.
All Rights for LION-HEARTED MUSIC Controlled and Administered by EMI APRIL MUSIC INC.
All Rights Reserved International Copyright Secured Used By Permission

F
Esus
E
F
I was in my room.
now it seems so sad.
bus-'ness left to do.
How was I to know.
Ev-'ry-thing he gave.
He nev-er said he loved.
To Coda
G7
1.
C
he thought I hung the moon?
to us took all he had.
me. Guess he
2.
C
Em
F
Then the days turned in-to years, and the
C
G
C
mem-'ries to black and white.
Em
F
He grew cold like an old win-ter wind
D.C. al Coda
C
G7sus
G7
blow-ing a-cross my life.
CODA
F
G
C
thought I knew.

GREEN GREEN GRASS OF HOME

Words and Music by
CURLY PUTMAN

Copyright © 1965 Sony Tree Publishing Co., Inc.
Copyright Renewed
All Rights Administered by Sony Music Publishing, 8 Music Square West, Nashville, TN 37203
International Copyright Secured All Rights Reserved

Additional Lyrics

2. The old house is still standing tho' the paint is cracked and dry,
And there's that old oak tree that I used to play on.
Down the lane I walk with my sweet Mary, hair of gold and lips like cherries:
It's good to touch the Green Green Grass Of Home.

3. Then I awake and look around me at the grey walls that surround me,
And I realize that I was only dreaming.
For there's a guard and there's a sad old Padre, arm in arm
we'll walk at daybreak,
Again I'll touch the Green Green Grass Of Home.

CHORUS:
Yes, they'll all come to see me in the shade of that old oak tree,
As they lay me 'neath the Green Green Grass Of Home.

HERE YOU COME AGAIN

Words by CYNTHIA WEIL
Music by BARRY MANN

© 1977 SCREEN GEMS-EMI MUSIC INC. and SUMMERHILL SONGS INC.
All Rights Controlled and Administered by SCREEN GEMS-EMI MUSIC INC.
All Rights Reserved International Copyright Secured Used by Permission

Em7/A
Dmaj7
D
C#m7
there go all my de - fens - es. Just
F#m7
F#m7/B
E
B/D#
C#m7
leave it up to you and in a lit - tle while you're
F#9
F#m7/B
mess-in' up my mind and fill-in' up my sens-es.
G
Gmaj7/B
C
Here You Come A - gain
(2nd time Instrumental)
G
Gmaj7/B
C
look-in' bet - ter than a bod - y has a right to: and
Em7
Am7
Em7
Am7
shak-in' me up so that all I real-ly know is
Am7/D
1.
2.
D7
here you come a-gain and here I go.
Cm7
Cm7/F
B♭maj7
B♭
All you got-ta do is smile that smile and

Fm7/Bb
E♭maj7
E♭
Dm7
there go all my de - fens - es. Just
Gm7
Gm7/C
F
C/E
Dm7
Dm7/C
leave it up to you and in a lit - tle while you're
G9
Gm7/C
mess-in' up my mind and fill-in' up my sens-es.
A♭
A♭maj7/C
D♭
Here You Come A - gain,
A♭
A♭maj7/C
D♭
look-in' bet - ter than a bod - y has a right to and
Fm7
B♭m7
Fm7
B♭m7
shak-in' me up so that all I real-ly know is
B♭m7/E♭
Here You Come A- gain and here I go
Repeat and Fade
A♭
A♭maj7/C
D♭
here I go

HARD ROCK BOTTOM OF YOUR HEART

Words and Music by
HUGH PRESTWOOD

Moderately fast country

Copyright © 1989 by Careers-BMG Music Publishing, Inc. and Hugh Prestwood Music
All Rights Administered by Careers-BMG Music Publishing, Inc.
International Copyright Secured All Rights Reserved

E A B
say - ing you can't e - ven start.
E A
And I feel like a stone you have
E B
picked up and thrown to the Hard
A B E
Rock Bot - tom Of Your Heart,
A B
to the Hard Rock Bot - tom Of Your Heart
1. 2.
E To Coda
Now this home
Bm A Bm
We can't just block it out. We've got to
A Bm A
talk it out un - til our hearts get back in
E Bm7 E
touch. I need your love, I miss it.

Bm7
E
F♯m
A
I can't go on like this, it hurts too
B
E
A
B
much.
(Instrumental)
D.S. al Coda
E
A
B
And I keep
CODA
A
B
To the Hard Rock Bot - tom Of Your Heart,
E
A
to the Hard Rock Bot -
B
E
A
- tom Of Your Heart.
B
E
A
B
E
A
E/B
B
Whoo, whoo,
E
A
B
Repeat and Fade
whoo.

HE STOPPED LOVING HER TODAY

Words and Music by BOBBY BRADDOCK
and CURLY PUTMAN

Moderately

G

1. He said, "I'll love you 'til I die,"
2. He kept some let - ters by his bed,
3. *(See additional lyrics)*

C

She told him, "You'll for - get in time."
dat - ed nine - teen - six - ty - two;

D7

As the years went slow - ly by,
He had un - der - lined in red

G

she still preyed up - on his mind;
ev - ery sin - gle "I love you";

$

He kept her pic - ture on his wall
I went to see him just to - day,

C

and went half - cra - zy now and then;
but I did - n't see no tears;

D7

But he still loved her through it all,
All dressed up to go a - way;

Copyright © 1978, 1980 Sony Tree Publishing Co., Inc.
All Rights Administered by Sony Music Publishing, 8 Music Square West, Nashville, TN 37203
International Copyright Secured All Rights Reserved

Additional Lyrics

(Recite)

3. She came to see him one last time
We all wondered if she would
And it kept running through my mind
This time he's over her for good.

THE HEART IS A LONELY HUNTER

Words and Music by KIM WILLIAMS,
ED HILL and MARK D. SANDERS

Moderately

G 3 D

She came in look - in' good _ and look-in' a - round.
She hears him say, "Hey, can _ I buy you a drink?"

G

She's check-in' out ev-'ry man _ in the room right
And sees the pale white _ cir-cle where he wears his

D Em

now. _ Don't go tell - in' her a-bout
ring. _ She knows he's deal-in' her a

G D Em

right or wrong; she's been a - lone _ for
dan-ger-ous hand, the con - se-quenc-es of

G A Asus A

way too _ long. _ Well, } The Heart _
a one-night stand. _ But, }

Copyright © 1993 Sony Cross Keys Publishing Co., Inc., Kim Williams Music,
New Haven Music, Inc., Music Hill Music, Starstruck Writers Group, Inc. and Mark D. Music
All Rights on behalf of Sony Cross Keys Publishing Co., Inc. and Kim Williams Music
Administered by Sony Music Publishing, 8 Music Square West, Nashville, TN 37203
All Rights on behalf of Music Hill Music Administered by New Haven Music, Inc.
International Copyright Secured All Rights Reserved

D
Is A Lone - ly Hunt - er with on -
D/F#
ly one de - sire: to find
G
some last - in' com - fort in the arms
Asus
A
of a lov - er's fire. Driv -
D
3
- en by a des - per - ate hun - ger to the dark
Bm7
of the ne - on light, oh, The Heart
G
Is A Lone - ly Hunt - er when there's no
A
1.
D N.C.
2.
D
sign of love in sight. sight.

Bm
A
From some-where deep in - side she tells him no.
G
Bm
Be-fore she starts to cry,
A
Gmaj9
A
N.C.
she turns to go.
Oh, The Heart
D
Is A Lone - ly Hunt - er with on -
D/F#
ly one de - sire: to find
G
some last - in' com - fort in the arms
Asus
Bbsus
of a lov - er's fire.
Driv-
Eb
3
- en by a des - per - ate hun - ger to the dark

Cm7
___ of the ne - on light, ___ oh, The Heart_
Ab
_____ Is A Lone - ly Hunt - er when there's no
Bb
Eb
sign of ___ love in ___ sight. Oh, The Heart_
Ab
_____ Is A Lone - ly Hunt - er when there's no
Bb
Eb N.C.
Cm
sign of love in sight. (Instrumental)
Eb
Gb
Ab
Eb

HERE'S A QUARTER
(Call Someone Who Cares)

Words and Music by
TRAVIS TRITT

Rowdy Country waltz (♫ = ♪♪)

Copyright © 1991 Tree Publishing Co., Inc. and Post Oak Publishing
All Rights Administered by Sony Music Publishing, 8 Music Square West, Nashville, TN 37203
International Copyright Secured All Rights Reserved

G
G7
C
Call some-one who'll
G
lis - ten and might give a
damn. May-be one of your
D
D7
sor - did af - fairs. But don't you
G
G7/B
come a - round here hand - ing me
C
G
none of your lines. Here's A
To Coda
D
Quar - ter. Call some - one who cares.
G
(Instrumental)

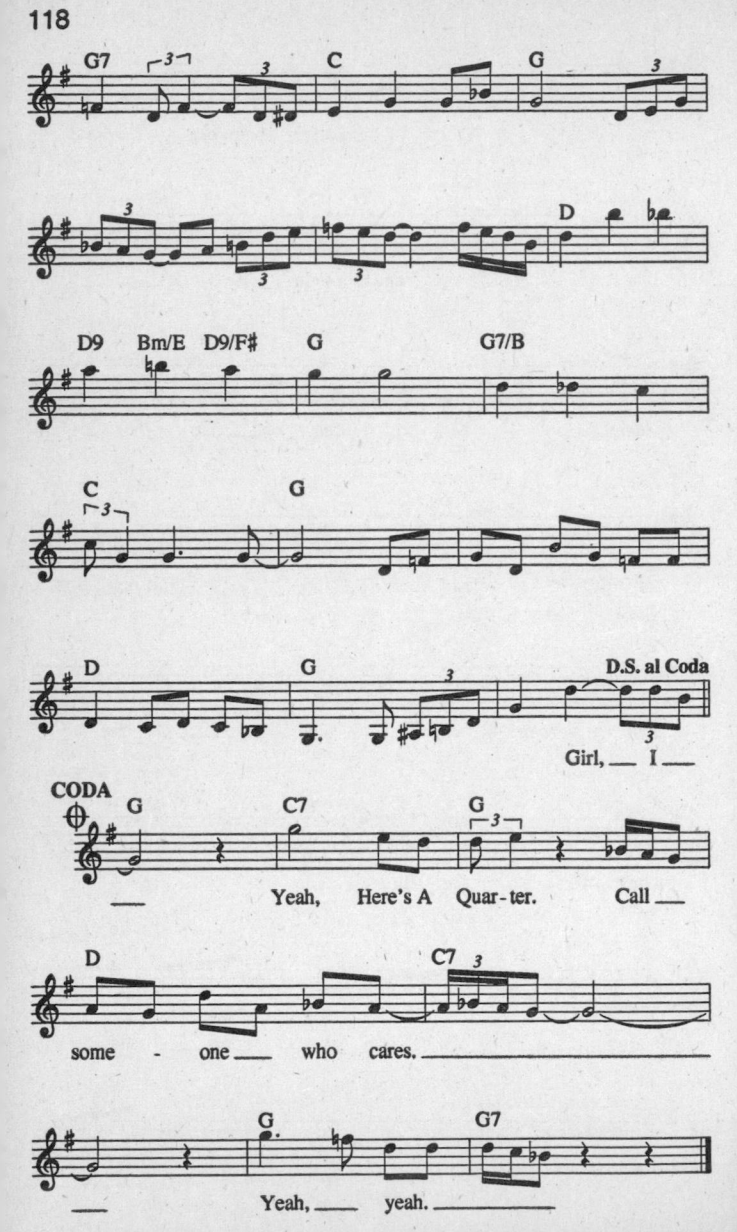
G7
C
G
D
D9
Bm/E
D9/F#
G
G7/B
C
G
D
G
D.S. al Coda
Girl, I
CODA
G
C7
G
Yeah, Here's A Quar-ter. Call
D
C7
some - one who cares.
G
G7
Yeah, yeah.

HOW CAN I HELP YOU SAY GOODBYE

Words and Music by BURTON COLLINS
and KAREN TAYLOR-GOOD

Copyright © 1993 Reynsong Publishing Corp., Burton B. Collins Publishing,
Howe Sound Music, W.B.M. Music Corp. and K.T. Good Music
All Rights for Burton B. Collins Publishing and Howe Sound Music Admininstered
by Reynsong Publishing Corp.
All Rights for K.T. Good Music Administered by W.B.M. Music Corp.
International Copyright Secured All Rights Reserved

F
F/G
G
Life's a-bout chang-ing; noth-ing ev-er stays the same." And she said,
C
G
C
"How can I help you to say good-bye? It's
Gsus
G
o-kay to hurt and it's o-kay to cry.
To Coda
F
G
C
C/E
F
Come let me hold you and I will try.
C/G
Am7
Gsus
G
How can I help you to say good-bye?"
Am7(add4)
G/B
1.
G/C C F/C C
D/G
G
I sat on our bed,
F
C
he packed his suit-case. I held a pic-ture of
Gsus
G
D/A
G/B
our wed-ding day. His hands were trem-blin',
F
C
we both were cry-in'. He kissed me gent-ly and then he

F/G G C F
quick-ly walked a - way. I called up Ma - ma. She said,
Gsus G F
"Time will ease your pain. Life's a-bout chang-ing; noth-ing
Gsus G
2. G/C C F/C C
ev - er stays the same." And she said, (Instrumental)
Am7 G/B F G/F F
F G/F F Gsus G
D.C. al Coda
CODA
F
C/G Am7 Gsus G
How can I help you to say
Am7(add4) G/B G/C C F/C C
good-bye?" (Instrumental)
Am7(add4) G/B G/C C F/C C

HEY, GOOD LOOKIN'

Words and Music by
HANK WILLIAMS

Copyright © 1951 by Hiriam Music and Acuff-Rose Music, Inc. in the U.S.A.
Copyright Renewed
All Rights for Hiriam Music Administered by Rightsong Music Inc.
All Rights outside the U.S.A. Controlled by Acuff-Rose Music, Inc.
International Copyright Secured All Rights Reserved

C
F
two dol - lar bill and I know a spot right
o - ver the fence and find me one for
C
F
o - ver the hill There's so - da pop and the
five or ten cents I'll keep it 'til it's
C
D7
danc - in's free, so if you wan - na have fun come a -
cov-ered with age 'Cause I'm writ - in' your name down on
G7
C
long with me Hey, Good Look - in'
ev - 'ry page Hey, Good Look - in'
What - cha got cook - in'
What - cha got cook - in'
D7
G7
How's a - bout cook - in' some - thin' up with
How's a - bout cook - in' some - thin' up with
1.
C
me.
I'm
2.
C F C
me.

I BELIEVE IN YOU

Words and Music by ROGER COOK
and SAM HOGIN

Moderately slow, triplet feel (♫ = ♩ ♪)

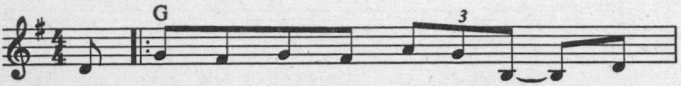

I don't be - lieve in su - per - stars, or
don't be - lieve that Heav - en waits for

gan - ic food and for - eign cars, I
on - ly those who con - gre - gate, I

don't be - lieve the price of gold, the
like to think of God as love, He's

cer - tain - ty of grow - ing old, that
down be - low, He's up a - bove, He's

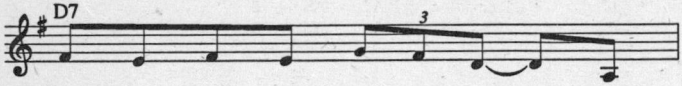

right is right and left is wrong, that
watch - ing peo - ple ev - 'ry - where, He

north and south can't get a - long, that
knows who does and does - n't care, and

© 1980 SCREEN GEMS-EMI MUSIC INC.
All Rights Reserved International Copyright Secured Used by Permission

G
east is east and west is west and
I'm an or - di - na - ry man, some -
be - ing first is al - ways best; but I be -
times I won - der who I am; but I be -
C
G
lieve in love;
lieve in love;
I be-lieve in ba - bies;
I be-lieve in mu - sic;
D7
I be-lieve in Mom and Dad and I Be-lleve In
I be-lieve in mag - ic and I Be-lieve In
1.
G
2.
G
You.
Well, I You.
C
I know with all my cer-tain-ty what's
G
go - in' on with you and me is a good thing.
D7
it's true; I be-lieve in
G
you. I don't be-lieve vir-gin-i-ty is as

com - mon as it used to be, in
work - in' days and sleep - in' nights, that
black is black and white is white, that
D7
Su - per - man and Rob - in Hood are
G
still a - live in Hol-ly-wood, that gas-o-line's in short sup-ply, the
C
ris - ing cost of get-tin' by; but I be - lieve in love;
lieve in love;
(Instrumental)
G
I be-lieve in old folks;
I be-lieve in ba - bies;
I be-lieve in
I be-lieve in
D7
1.
G
chil - dren;
Mom and Dad
I Be-lieve In You.
2.
G
D.S. and Fade
I be - and I Be-lieve In You.

I FEEL LUCKY

Words and Music by MARY CHAPIN CARPENTER
and DON SCHLITZ

Well, I woke up this morn - ing, stum - bled
strolled down to the cor - ner, gave my
lev - en mil - lion lat - er, I was

out of my rack. I o - pened up the pa - per to the
num-bers to the clerk. The pot's e - lev - en mil-lion, so I
sit - tin' at the bar. I bought the house a dou-ble, then the

page in the back. It on - ly took a min-ute for my
called in sick to work. I bought a pack of Cam-els, a bur -
wait-ress a new car. Dwight Yoa-kam's in the cor-ner,

fin-ger to find my dai - ly dose of des-tin - y un -
ri - to and a Barks, crossed a - gainst the light, made a
try'n to catch my eye. Lyle Lov-ett's right be - side me with his

- der my sign. My eyes just a - bout popped
bee - line for the park. The sky be-gan to thun-der, the
hand up - on my thigh. The mor-al of this sto - ry, it's

© 1992 EMI APRIL MUSIC INC., GETAREALJOB MUSIC and DON SCHLITZ MUSIC
All Rights for GETAREALJOB MUSIC Controlled and Administered by EMI APRIL MUSIC INC.
All Rights Administered by ALMO MUSIC CORP. on behalf of DON SCHLITZ MUSIC
All Rights Reserved International Copyright Secured Used by Permission

out - a my head. It said, "The
wind be - gan to moan. I heard a
sim - ple but it's true: hey, the
B
N.C.
stars are stacked a - gainst you girl.
voice a - bove me say - in', "Girl you'd
stars might lie, but the
E7
Get back in bed."
bet-ter get back home."
num - bers nev-er do.
I Feel Luck - y,
B7
To Coda
I Feel Luck-y, yeah.
No
No
F#7
Pro - fes - sor Doom gon - na stand in my way.
trop - i - cal de - pres-sion gon - na steal my sun a - way.
B N.C.
1.
B7
Mm, I Feel Luck-y to-day.
2.
E7
Well, I Luck-y to - day.
(Instrumental)
B7

F#7
B7
F#
D.S. al Coda
Now e -
CODA
F#7
Hey Dwight, hey Lyle, boys,
B7
you don't have to fight.
Hot dog, I Feel
E7
Luck-y to-night. I Feel Luck-y,
B7
I Feel Luck-y, yeah.
F#7
Think I'll flip a coin, I'm a
B N.C.
win-ner ei-ther way.
Mm, I Feel
C#9 C9 B9
Luck-y to-day.

I CAN LOVE YOU LIKE THAT

Words and Music by STEVE DIAMOND,
MARIBETH DERRY and JENNIFER KIMBALL

Moderate Ballad

They read you Cin-der-el - la, you hoped it would come true that
nev - er make a prom-ise I don't in - tend to keep. So,

one day your Prince Charm-ing would come res-cue you. You
when I say for - ev - er, for - ev - er's what I mean.

like ro-man-tic mov-ies; you nev-er will for-get the
I'm no Ca-sa-no-va, but I swear this much is true:

way you felt when Ro-me-o kissed Ju-li-et.
I'll be hold-ing noth-ing back when it comes to you. You

All this time that you've been wait - ing,
dream of love that's ev - er - last - ing. Well,

© 1995 Diamond Cuts, Criterion Music Corp., Full Keel Music Co.,
Second Wave Music and Friends And Angels Music
All Rights for Diamond Cuts in the U.S. and Canada Administered by Wonderland Music Company, Inc.
All Rights for Second Wave Music and Friends And Angels Music Administered by Full Keel Music Co.
International Copyright Secured All Rights Reserved

Em7
F
you don't have to wait no more.
ba - by, o - pen up your eyes.
G7sus
C
I Can Love You Like That.
I would make you my world,
Em
F
move heav-en and earth
if you were my girl.
G7sus
C
I will give you my heart,
be all that you need,
Em
F
show you you're ev - 'ry-thing that's pre-cious to me.
Bb
If you give me a chance,
1.
G7sus
C
F
G7sus
I Can Love You Like That.
I
2.
C
Gm7
You want ten-der-ness, I got ten -

Dm7
C
- der-ness. And I see through to the
Gm7
Dm7
heart of you. If you want a man who un - der-stands,
F
G7sus
you don't have to look ver - y far.
G
I can love you, I can, I Can Love You Like That.
C
Em
I would make you my world, move heav-en and earth
F
G7sus
if you were my girl. I will give you my heart,
C
Em
be all that you need, show you you're ev -
Repeat and Fade
F
G7sus
- 'ry-thing that's pre-cious to me. I Can Love You Like That.

I NEVER KNEW LOVE

Words and Music by WILL ROBINSON
and LARRY BOONE

Moderately

G D Em7

I nev-er knew the pow - er ___ of a song___
I nev-er un - der-stood the mean-ing of home _

Em/D C D

till I heard the mu - sic play - in' the day
till I pulled in - to _ that old dirt drive af - ter

C/G G C/G G

Mom-ma passed on. ___ Nev-er knew what
be - ing gone too long. _ I did-n't know what se -

D Em7 G7

in - no - cence _ was a - bout ___ till the
ren - i - ty ___ real - ly was ___ till I

C D C/G G

first time I ___ laid eyes _ on the face _ of a new - born child._
stopped one day_ to lis - ten to ___ that ol' riv-er gen - tly run. _

© 1993 Wonderland Music Company, Inc., Will Robinsongs and Sony Cross Keys Publishing Co., Inc.
All Rights on behalf of Will Robinsongs Administered by Wonderland Music Company, Inc.,
500 S. Buena Vista St., Burbank, CA 91521
All Rights on behalf of Sony Cross Keys Publishing Co., Inc. Administered by Sony Music Publishing,
8 Music Square West, Nashville, TN 37203
International Copyright Secured All Rights Reserved

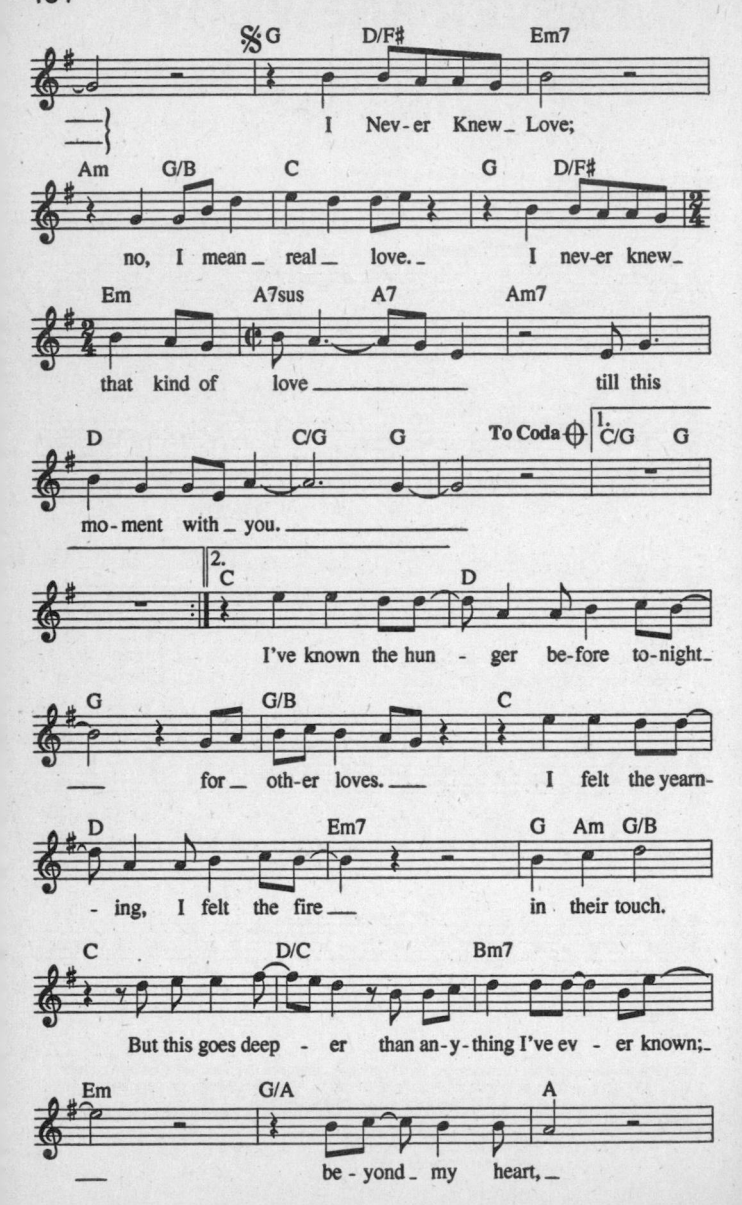
G D/F# Em7
I Nev-er Knew_ Love;
Am G/B C G D/F#
no, I mean_ real_ love._ I nev-er knew_
Em A7sus A7 Am7
that kind of love_____ till this
D C/G G To Coda 1. C/G G
mo-ment with_ you._____
2. C D
I've known the hun - ger be-fore to-night_
G G/B C
___ for_ oth-er loves.___ I felt the yearn-
D Em7 G Am G/B
- ing, I felt the fire___ in their touch.
C D/C Bm7
But this goes deep - er than an-y-thing I've ev - er known;_
Em G/A A
___ be - yond_ my heart,_

Am7 G/B C D G
clear down to my soul.
D Em G/D
(Instrumental)
C D C/G G
D/F#
I nev-er knew what beau-ty could be -
Em7 G7 G7/B C
hold till you looked at me and
D C/G G
I could see for - ev - er un - fold.
C/G G
D.S. al Coda
Oh, you made me whole
CODA
Am7 D C/G G
Till I was loved by you.
C/G G
(Instrumental)

I FALL TO PIECES

Words and Music by HANK COCHRAN
and HARLAN HOWARD

Copyright © 1960 Tree Publishing Co., Inc.
Copyright Renewed
All Rights Administered by Sony Music Publishing, 8 Music Square West, Nashville, TN 37203
International Copyright Secured All Rights Reserved

___ You want me to act like we've
___ You tell me to find some - one

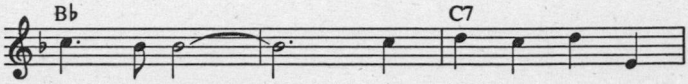

nev - er kissed; ___ you want me to for -
else to love, ___ some - one who'll love me,

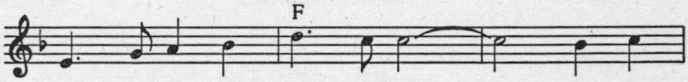

get, pre-tend we've nev - er met; ___ And I've
too, the way you used to do; ___ But each

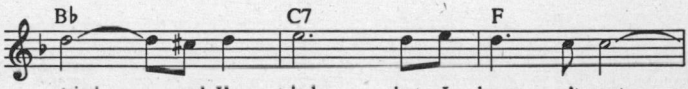

tried ___ and I've tried, but I have - n't yet; ___
time ___ I go out with ___ some - one new; ___

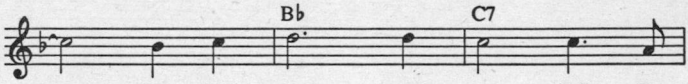

___ You walk by and I Fall To
___ You walk by and I Fall To

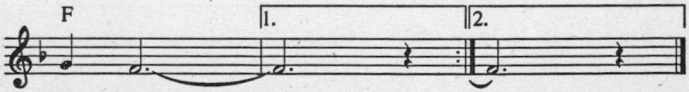

Piec - es. ___
Piec - es. ___ ___

I JUST FALL IN LOVE AGAIN

Words and Music by LARRY HERBSTRITT, STEPHEN H. DORFF, GLORIA SKLEROV and HARRY LLOYD

Copyright © 1977 by Careers-BMG Music Publishing, Inc. and BMG Songs, Inc.
International Copyright Secured All Rights Reserved

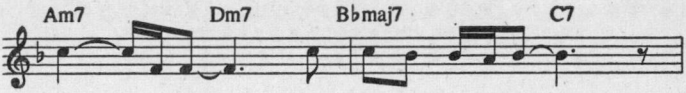
Am7 Dm7 B♭maj7 C7
oh, I Just Fall In Love A - gain.

Fsus F Dm7 G9 C6 C
Just one touch and then it hap - pens ev - 'ry time. And there I

Am7 Dm7 B♭maj7 Em7♭5 A7♭9
go, I Just Fall In Love A - gain, and when I

Dm7 G7 F B♭
do I can't help my - self I fall in love with

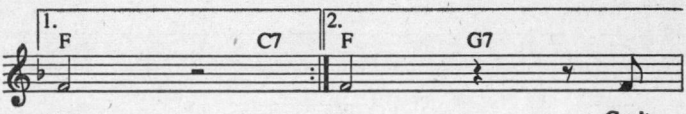
1.
F C7
2.
F G7
you.
you.
Can't

F B♭ F
help my - self I fall in love with you.

I WOULDN'T HAVE MISSED IT FOR THE WORLD

Words and Music by KYE FLEMING,
DENNIS MORGAN and CHARLES QUILLEN

Moderately Fast

Am7 G

1. Our paths may nev-er cross a - gain;
2. *(See additional lyrics)*

Cmaj7

may-be my heart will nev - er mend,

G Em7

but I'm glad for

C

all the good times. You brought me so

Am7

much sun - shine, and love was the best

D Bm7

it's ev - er been.

𝄋 **Chorus**

G C

I Would-n't Have Missed It For The World;

Copyright © 1981 Songs Of PolyGram International, Inc. and PolyGram International Publishing, Inc.
International Copyright Secured All Rights Reserved

Additional Lyrics

2. They say that all good things must end.
Love comes and goes just like the wind.
You've got your dreams to follow,
But if I had the chance tomorrow,
You know I'd do it all again.
(CHORUS)

I'LL STILL BE LOVING YOU

Words and Music by TODD CERNEY, PAM ROSE, MARYANN KENNEDY and PAT BUNCH

© Copyright 1986 by MCA MUSIC PUBLISHING, A Division of MCA INC., CHRISWALD MUSIC, INC., HOPI SOUND MUSIC, WARNER-TAMERLANE PUBLISHING CORP., FLAMINGO ROSE MUSIC and CHOY LA RUE MUSIC
All Rights for CHRISWALD MUSIC, INC. and HOPI SOUND MUSIC Controlled and Administered by MCA MUSIC PUBLISHING, A Division of MCA INC.
All Rights for FLAMINGO ROSE MUSIC and CHOY LA RUE MUSIC Administered by WARNER-TAMERLANE PUBLISHING CORP.
International Copyright Secured All Rights Reserved

MCA music publishing

C#m7
C
G
stands still,
un - til the winds don't blow.
A
F#m7
C#m7
When to-day is just a mem-ry to me, I know
C
G
C
G
D
To Coda
I'll still be lov-in', I'll Still Be Lov-in' You.
1.
C
I'll Still Be Lov - in' You.
Nev-er be-fore
2.
E
F#/A#
(Instrumental)
Amaj7
B
E
F#/A#
G#m
G
D
E
D.S. al Coda
CODA
C
D
I'll Still Be Lov - in' You.
I'll still be lov-in',
C
Repeat and Fade
I'll Still Be Lov-in' You. I'll Still Be Lov-in' You.

I'M NOT LISA

Words and Music by
JESSI COLTER

Copyright © 1972 Songs Of PolyGram International, Inc.
International Copyright Secured All Rights Reserved

F Bb/F F Bb/F F
day, his hand led her a - way. She left you
F7
here drown - ing in your tears,
here where you've stayed for years, cry - ing
Bb C7
Li - sa, Li -
F
sa. I'm Not Li - sa, My name is
not blue, but mine won't
Bb C7
Ju - lie; Li - sa left you
leave you 'til the sun - light
1. F C7
years a - go. My eyes are
2. F
shines through your face. I'm Not Li - sa.

I'VE COME TO EXPECT IT FROM YOU

Words and Music by DEAN DILLON
and BUDDY CANNON

Moderate two-beat

G

1. So up - set, A ner - vous wreck.
2. mil - lion times, A mil - lion lines
3. *(Instrumental)*
4. could raise hell, But what the hell,

C

Can't be - lieve you said good - bye.
and I bought 'em ev - 'ry - one.
(Instrumental)
it would-n't do a bit of good.

(Instrumental)

G

Sit and smoke, cry and joke
You don't care. You rip and
(Instrumental)
Pack and leave, my heart a -

C

a - bout these tears in my eyes.
tear ev - 'ry dream I've count - ed on.
(Instrumental)
grees it seems to think that I should.

© Copyright 1990 by MUSIC CORPORATION OF AMERICA, INC., JESSIE JO MUSIC,
BUDDY CANNON MUSIC and POLYGRAM INTERNATIONAL PUBLISHING, INC.
All Rights for JESSIE JO MUSIC Controlled and Administered by MUSIC CORPORATION OF AMERICA, INC.
International Copyright Secured All Rights Reserved
MCA music publishing

(Instrumental)
Am
1.,3. How could you do what you've
2. I guess that I should thank my
4. There won't be no more
G#+
gone and done to me?
un - luck - y star
next time do - in' me wrong.
C/G
I would-n't treat a dog the way
that I'm a - live and
You'll come back this time to find
D
you treat - ed me.
you're the way you are.
out that I'm gone.
G7
But that's what I get.
But that's what I get.
But that's what I get.

C
I've Come To Ex - pect It From You.
I've Come To Ex - pect It From You.
you should ex - pect it from me.
(Instrumental)
1.,2.,3.
2. A
4. I
4.
G7
That's what I
get.
I've Come To Ex - pect
C
It From You.
(Instrumental)

LOOKIN' FOR LOVE

Words and Music by WANDA MALLETTE,
PATTI RYAN and BOB MORRISON

© 1980 TEMI COMBINE INC. and SOUTHERN DAYS MUSIC
All Rights for TEMI COMBINE INC. Controlled by MUSIC CITY MUSIC INC. and
Administered by EMI APRIL MUSIC INC.
All Rights Reserved International Copyright Secured Used by Permission

D
Look-in' For Love in all the wrong plac - es,
Look-in' For Love in all the wrong plac - es,
Look-in' For Love in all the wrong plac - es,
F#m
Look-in' For Love in too man - y fac - es,
Look-in' For Love in too man - y fac - es,
Look-in' For Love in too man - y fac - es,
G
search-in' their eyes and look-in' for trac - es of
search-in' their eyes and look-in' for trac - es of
search-in' their eyes and look-in' for trac - es of
Em F#m G A D
what I'm dream-in' of. Hop-in' to find a friend
what I'm dream-in' of. Hop-in' to find a friend
what I'm dream-in' of. Now that I've found a friend
To Coda
F#m
and a lov - er; I'll bless the day I dis-cov-er an-
and a lov - er; I'll bless the day I dis-cov-er an-
and a lov - er; I bless the day I dis-cov-ered
G Em A
1. D
oth-er heart Look-in' For Love.
oth-er heart Look-in' For Love.
2. D
G
Then you came a knock - in' at

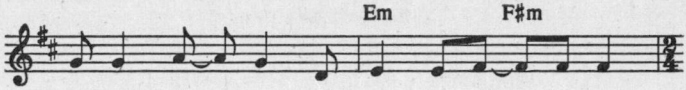
Em
F♯m
my heart's door; you're ev - 'ry - thing I've been

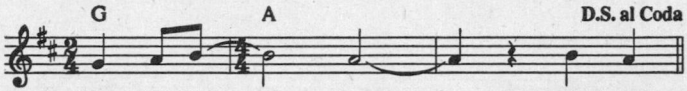
G
A
D.S. al Coda
look - in' for. No more

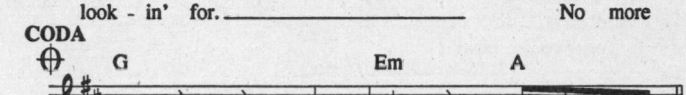
CODA
G
Em
A
you, oh you; Look-in' For Love.

D
F♯m
in all the wrong plac-es; in too.

G
man - y fac - es, search-in' their eyes and

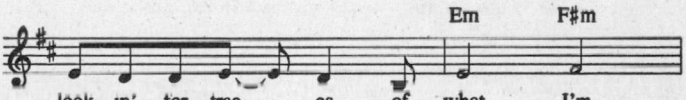
Em
F♯m
look - in' for trac - es of what I'm

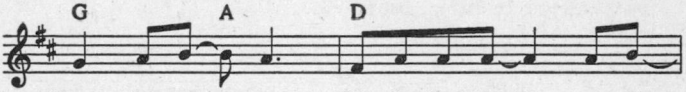
G
A
D
dream - in' of. Now that I've found a friend.

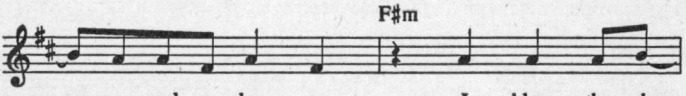
F♯m
and a lov - er; I bless the day.

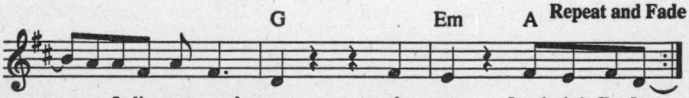
G
Em
A
Repeat and Fade
I dis-cov-ered you, oh you; Look-in' For Love.

I.O.U.

Words and Music by KERRY CHATER
and AUSTIN ROBERTS

Copyright © 1982 SONGS OF POLYGRAM INTERNATIONAL, INC. and MCA MUSIC PUBLISHING,
A Division of MCA INC.
International Copyright Secured All Rights Reserved
MCA music publishing

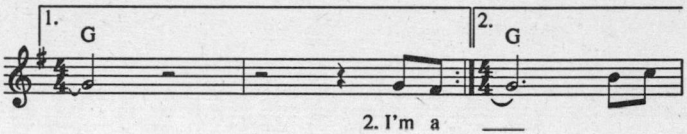

Additional Lyrics

2. I'm amazed
When you say it's me you live for
And you know that when I'm holding you
You're right where you belong
And my love
I can't help but smile with wonder
When you tell me what I've done for you
'Cause I've known all along
That....*(CHORUS)*

IT'S A HEARTACHE

Words and Music by RONNIE SCOTT
and STEVE WOLFE

Copyright © 1978 by Lojo Music Ltd. and Careers-BMG Music Publishing, Inc.
All Rights Administered by Careers-BMG Music Publishing, Inc.
International Copyright Secured All Rights Reserved

F
It ain't wise to need some -
G/D
Em
one as much as I de-pend - ed on
A/E
G
To Coda
D.S. al Coda
you.
4. Oh It's A
CODA
C
Oh, It's A Heart - ache,
fool's game,
Em
noth - ing but a heart - ache.
noth - ing but a fool's game,
F
You love him 'til your arms break,
stand-ing in the cold rain,
C
Repeat and Fade
then he'll let you down.
feel - ing like a clown.
It's A

IT'S NOW OR NEVER

Words and Music by AARON SCHROEDER
and WALLY GOLD

Copyright (for the U.S.A.) © 1960 by Gladys Music, Inc.
U.S.A. Copyright Renewed and Assigned to Gladys Music (Administered by Williamson Music)
and Rachel's Own Music (Administered by A. Schroeder International Ltd.); rights for all countries
in the world (except U.S.A.) owned by Edizioni Bideri S.p.A, Naples
International Copyright Secured All Rights Reserved

INTERLUDE
Eb
Fine
Eb
wait.
saw you.
wil - low
Eb+ Ab
with your smile so ten - der, My heart was
we could cry an o - cean, If we lost
Bb7 Ebm6 Eb
cap - tured; my soul sur - ren - dered.
true love and sweet de - vo - tion.
N.C. Eb Eb+
I've spent a life - time wait-ing for the
Your lips ex - cite me; let your arms in -
Ab Abm Eb Ebdim
right time Now that you're near the time is
vite me. For who knows when we'll meet a -
Fm7 Bb7 Eb Abm Eb N.C.
here at last.
gain this way.
It's Now Or

JAMBALAYA
(On The Bayou)

Words and Music by
HANK WILLIAMS

Copyright © 1952 by Hiriam Music and Acuff-Rose Music, Inc. in the U.S.A.
Copyright Renewed
All Rights for Hiriam Music Administered by Rightsong Music Inc.
All Rights outside the U.S.A. Controlled by Acuff-Rose Music, Inc.
International Copyright Secured All Rights Reserved

Additional Lyrics

3. Settle down far from town, get me a pirogue,
And I'll catch all the fish in the bayou,
Swap my mon to buy Yvonne what she need-o,
Son of a gun, we'll have big fun on the bayou.

THE KEEPER OF THE STARS

Words and Music by DICKEY LEE, DANNY MAYO and KAREN STALEY

Copyright © 1994 Songs Of PolyGram International, Inc., Pal Time Music, Sixteen Stars Music, New Haven Music, Inc. and Murrah Music Corp.
International Copyright Secured All Rights Reserved

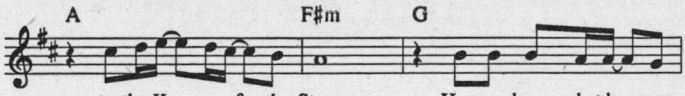
A
F#m
G
to the Keep-er of_ the Stars.
He sure knew what he_was

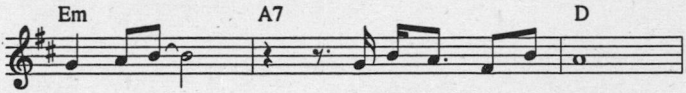
Em
A7
D
do - in'__
when he joined these two hearts.

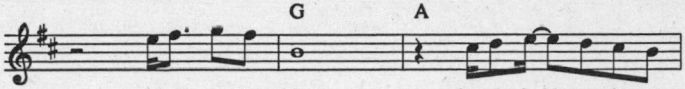
G
A
I hold ev-'ry-thing
when I hold_you in my

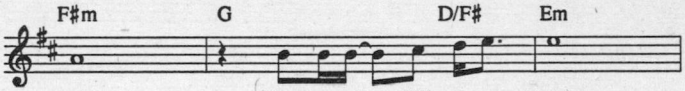
F#m
G
D/F#
Em
arms.
I've got all__ I'll ev-er need,

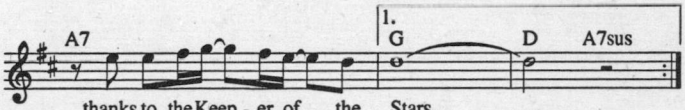
A7
1.
G
D
A7sus
thanks to the Keep-er of__ the Stars.

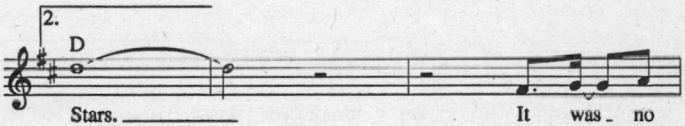
2.
D
Stars.
It was_ no

A/C#
Bm
G
ac-ci-dent,__
me find-ing you.

D/F#
Some-one had a hand in it__

Em
A7
D
A7sus
D
long be-fore_ we ev-er knew.

KENTUCKY RAIN

Words and Music by EDDIE RABBITT
and DICK HEARD

Slowly (triplet feel)

C G C F

Sev - en lone - ly days and a doz - en towns a - go, I
Showed your pho - to - graph to some old gray beard - ed men Sitting

C F C C7

reached out one night and you were gone;
on a bench out - side a gen - 'ral store; They said,

F G C Am

Don't know why you'd run, what you're run - nin' to or _ from,
"Yes, _ she's been here," but their mem - 'ry _ was - n't clear, Was it

D7 G7

All I know is I want to bring you home. _____ So I'm
yes - ter - day, no _ wait, the day be - fore. _____

C G C F

walk - ing _ in the rain, thumb - ing _ for a ride, _ On this
Fi - n'ly _ got a ride with a preach - er _ man who asked, _ "Where you

C F C C7

lone - ly _____ Ken - tuck - y back road. _____ I've
bound on such a dark _ aft - er - noon?" _____ As we

Copyright © 1970 by Elvis Presley Music, Inc. and S-P-R Music Corp.
Copyright Assigned to Elvis Presley Music and Careers-BMG Music Publishing, Inc.
All Rights Administered by R&H Music
International Copyright Secured All Rights Reserved

F G C Am
loved you much too long and my love's too strong, To
drove on thru the rain, as he lis-tened, I ex-plained, And he
D7 G7
let you go, nev-er know-ing what went wrong.
left me with a prayer that I'd find you.
Fmaj7 D7 C Bm
Ken-tuck-y Rain keeps pour-ing down,
Em Am7 F Em
And up a-head's an-oth-er town that I'll go
F C Fmaj7 C Em
walk-ing thru, With the rain in my shoes,
Am Em C Am Am7 F6
Search-ing for you,
G7 C Em
In the cold Ken-tuck-y Rain,
F G7 1. C Dm7 G7
In the cold Ken-tuck-y Rain.
2. C Em F Repeat and Fade
Rain, In the cold Ken-tuck-y

KING OF THE ROAD

Words and Music by
ROGER MILLER

Copyright © 1964 Sony Tree Publishing Co., Inc.
Copyright Renewed
This arrangement Copyright © 1995 Sony Tree Publishing Co., Inc.
All Rights Administered by Sony Music Publishing, 8 Music Square West, Nashville, TN 37203
International Copyright Secured All Rights Reserved

F
man of means by no means
To Coda
1.
C
G
King Of The Road.
2.
C
Road I know ev - er - y en - gi - neer on
F
G
ev - er - y train all of the chil - dren and
C
all of their names And ev - er - y hand - out in
F
G
ev - er - y town and ev - 'ry lock that ain't locked when
D.C. (1st verse) al Coda
no one's a - round. I sing
CODA
C
Road.

LAY DOWN SALLY

Words and Music by ERIC CLAPTON,
MARCY LEVY and GEORGE TERRY

Copyright © 1977 by Eric Patrick Clapton and Throat Music Ltd.
All Rights for the U.S. Administered by Unichappell Music Inc.
International Copyright Secured All Rights Reserved

E
And don't you ev - er leave.
And don't you ev - er leave.
And don't you ev - er leave.
A
D
Lay Down, Sal - ly, and rest you in my arms.
E
Don't you think you want some - one to talk
A
to? Lay Down, Sal -
D
ly; no need to leave so soon.
E
To Coda
I've been try - ing all night long just to
1.,2.
A
3.
A
D.S. al Coda
talk to you.
2. The talk to you.
3. I
CODA
A
talk to you.

LOST IN THE FIFTIES TONIGHT

(In The Still Of The Nite)

Words and Music by MIKE REID,
TROY SEALS and FRED PARRIS

Copyright © 1984 by BMG Songs, Inc., WB Music Corp., Two Sons Music and Llee Corp.
International Copyright Secured All Rights Reserved

F
Dm
still of the night, hold me
Bb
C
dar ling, hold me tight. Oh,
F
Dm
shoo-doop, shoo-be do. Shoo-doop, doo; so
Bb
C
1.
F
real, so right, lost in the feel-ing to-night.
A
Bb
C
2.
F
night.
F
Dm
Shoo-doop, shoo-be doo, shoo-doop, shoo-be doo,
Bb
C
Repeat ad lib. and Fade
shoo-doop, shoo-be doo, shoo-doop, shoo-be, doo.

LOVE WITHOUT END, AMEN

Words and Music by
AARON G. BARKER

Moderately, with a beat

Copyright © 1990 O-Tex Music (BMI) and Bill Butler Music (BMI), 1000 18th Avenue South,
Nashville, TN 37212
International Copyright Secured All Rights Reserved

A
D
wait-ed for the worst. And he said,
passed it on to him. I said,
G
D
"Let me tell you a se-cret a-bout a fa-ther's love, a
se-cret that my Dad-dy said was just be-tween us."
A
A7
G
A7
He said, I said, "Dad-dies don't just love their chil-dren
D
D/F#
G
ev-'ry now and then, it's a
D
A
Love With-out End, A - men."
D
A
It's a Love With-out End, A - men.

1.
2.
D
D
B7
(Instrumental) When (Instrumental) Last
E
A
night I dreamed I died and stood out - side those pearl-y gates.
E
When sud-den-ly, I re-al - ized there
B7
must be some mis-take. If
A
B7
E
E/G#
they knew half the things I've done they'll nev-er let me in.
A
E
And then some-where from the oth-er side I
B7
E
heard these words a - gain. And they said,

A
E
"Let me tell_you a se - cret _ a - bout _ a fa - ther's_ love, a
se - cret that _ my _____ Dad - dy said _____ was
B
just be - tween __ us."
You see,
A
B
E
E/G#
A
Dad - dies just_don't love_their chil - dren ev - 'ry now_and then, __
E
B
it's a Love With - out End, __ A - men.
E
B
It's a Love With - out End, __ A - men.
E
(Instrumental)

LUCILLE

Words and Music by ROGER BOWLING
and HAL BYNUM

© 1976 ATV MUSIC CORP. and ANDITE INVASION MUSIC
All Rights for ATV MUSIC CORP. Controlled and Administered by EMI BLACKWOOD MUSIC INC.
under license from ATV MUSIC CORP.
All Rights Reserved International Copyright Secured Used by Permission

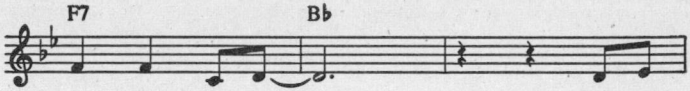

asked her her name. When the
look on his face. The

drinks fin - 'ly hit her, she said, "I'm no
big hands were cal - loused, he looked like a

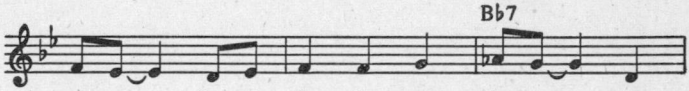

quit - ter, but I fin - 'ly quit liv - ing on
moun-tain, for a min - ute I thought I was

dreams. I'm hun - gry for
dead. But he start - ed

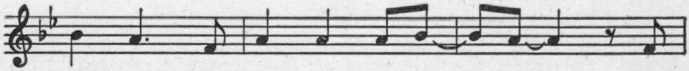

laugh - ter and here ev - er - af - ter, I'm
shak - ing, his big heart was break - ing, he

af - ter what-ev - er the oth - er life

brings." In the turned to the

B♭
wom - an ___ and said: "You picked a
E♭
fine time to leave ___ me, Lu - cille,
with four hun - gry chil - dren and a
B♭
crop in the field.
E♭
I've had some bad times, ___ lived through some
sad times, ___ but this time ___ your hurt - in' won't
B♭
F7
heal, You picked a fine time to

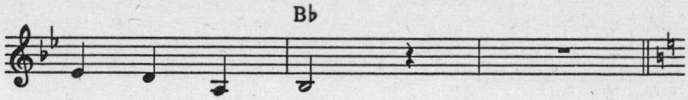
B♭
leave me, Lu - cille."

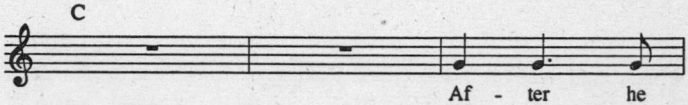
C
Af - ter he

left us I or - dered more whis - key, I

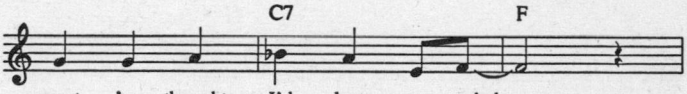
C7
F
must - 've thought I'd lost my mind;

G7
I could - n't hold her 'cause the

words that he told her kept com - ing back

C
N.C.
time af - ter time:
You picked a

F
fine time to leave me, Lu - cille,
with four hun - gry chil - dren and a
C
crop in the field.
F
I've had some bad times, lived through some
sad times, but this time your hurt - in' won't
C
G7
heal, you picked a fine time to
Repeat and Fade
C
N.C.
leave me, Lu - cille.
You picked a

MAMMAS DON'T LET YOUR BABIES GROW UP TO BE COWBOYS

Words and Music by ED BRUCE
and PATSY BRUCE

Copyright © 1975 Sony Tree Publishing Co., Inc.
This arrangement Copyright © 1995 Sony Tree Publishing Co., Inc.
All Rights Administered by Sony Music Publishing, 8 Music Square West, Nashville, TN 37203
International Copyright Secured All Rights Reserved

B♭
Up To Be Cow - boys,
C7
'Cause they'll nev - er stay home, and they're
al - ways a - lone, E - ven with
F
Fine
some - one they love.
F
1. A cow-boy ain't eas - y to
2. (See additional lyrics)
B♭
love, and he's hard - er to hold.
C7
And it means more to him to
give you a song than sil - ver or
F
gold.

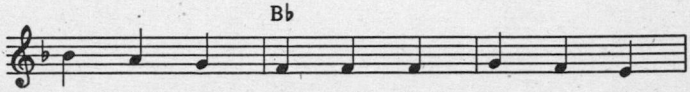

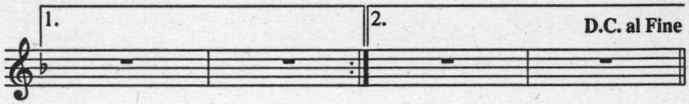

Additional Lyrics

2. A cowboy loves smokey ole pool rooms and clear mountain mornings,
Little warm puppies and children and girls of the night.
Them that don't know him won't like him and them that do sometimes won't know how to take him.
He's not wrong he's just different and his pride won't let him do things to make you think he's right.
(CHORUS)

NEON MOON

Words and Music by
RONNIE DUNN

Copyright © 1990 Tree Publishing Co., Inc. and Showbilly Music
All Rights Administered by Sony Music Publishing, 8 Music Square West, Nashville, TN 37203
International Copyright Secured All Rights Reserved

ta - ble for two — way in back — where
how man - y lies — that I've lied — tell - ing
words of ev - 'ry sad song seem to say what I think. And this

I sit a - lone — and think of
my poor — heart — she'll come
hurt in-side of me ain't nev-er

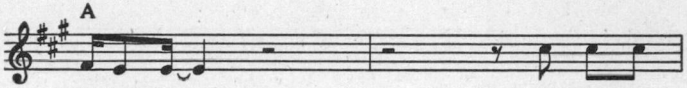

los-ing you. — I spend most
back some day. — Oh, but I'll
gon-na end. — Oh, but I'll

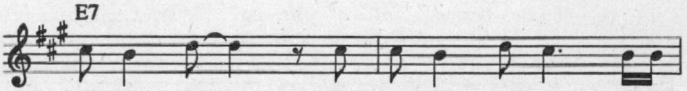

ev - 'ry night — be - neath the light — of a
be al - right — as long as there's light from a
be al - right — as long as there's light from a

Ne - on Moon. — Now if you
Ne - on Moon. — Oh, — if you
Ne - on Moon. — Oh, — if you

lose — your one — and on - ly, there's al-ways

D
E
room here for the lone - ly to watch your
D
E
bro-ken dreams dance in and out of the beams of a
A
1.,2.
Ne - on Moon. I think of
3.
A(add9)
E
Come watch your bro - ken dreams dance in and
A
out of the beams of a Ne - on Moon.
E
Oh, watch your bro-ken dreams dance in and
out of the beams of a
A
Ne - on Moon.
A(add9)
Repeat and Fade

SHE BELIEVES IN ME

Words and Music by
STEVE GIBB

Copyright © 1977 PolyGram International Publishing, Inc.
International Copyright Secured All Rights Reserved

Gm7
Cm
F7
come to her and say it was all right.
And I
Bb
F7sus
hold her tight.
And She Be -
Bbsus
Bb
Bbsus
Bb
lieves In Me.
I'll nev - er know just what she
Am7b5
D7
sees in me.
I told her some - day if she
Gm
Gm(maj7)
Gm7
Gm6
was my girl
I could change the world
with my
Cm7
F7sus
lit - tle songs,
I was wrong.
But she has
Bbsus
Bb
Bbsus
Bb
faith in me,
And so I go on try - ing

Am7b5
D7
faith - ful-ly, _
And who knows, may - be ___ on some
Gm
Gm(maj7)
Gm7
Gm6
spe-cial night _
If my song is right
I will
Cm7
F7sus
find ___ a way, _
find a way.
While she lays
Bb
Bb/D
wait - ing ___
I stum-ble to the kitch - en ___ for a
Eb
Cm7
F7
F/Eb
bite. ___
Then I see my old gui-tar in ___ the
Dm7
Gm(maj7)
Gm7
night,
just wait-ing for me like ___ a se-cret
Cm7
F7sus
friend,
And there's no end.
While she lays

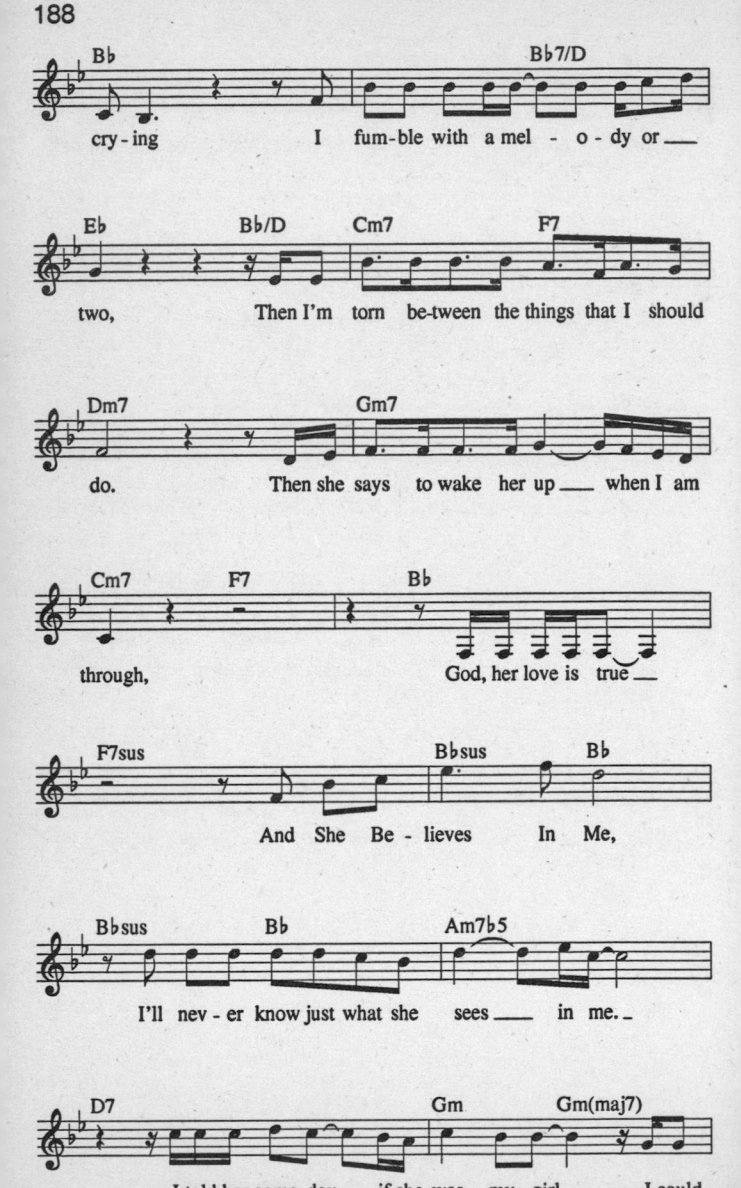
Bb
Bb7/D
cry - ing I fum - ble with a mel - o - dy or
Eb
Bb/D
Cm7
F7
two, Then I'm torn be-tween the things that I should
Dm7
Gm7
do. Then she says to wake her up when I am
Cm7
F7
Bb
through, God, her love is true
F7sus
Bbsus
Bb
And She Be - lieves In Me,
Bbsus
Bb
Am7b5
I'll nev - er know just what she sees in me.
D7
Gm
Gm(maj7)
I told her some-day if she was my girl I could

change the world _ with my lit-tle songs, _ I was

wrong. But she has faith ___ in me, _

And so I go on try - ing faith - ful-ly, _

And, who knows, may-be __ on some spe-cial night _ If my

song is right I will find ___ a way, _

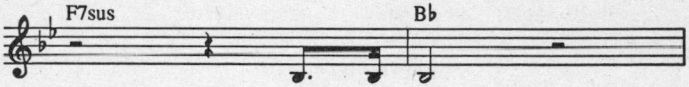

while she waits,

while ____ she waits, for me.

NO ONE ELSE ON EARTH

Words and Music by SAM LORBER,
STEWART HARRIS and JILL COLUCCI

Medium Blues feel

G C F C

I've been a rock and I've got my fenc - es,
You can make me want you ___ an-y-time you want to,
D.S. *Instrumental*

G C F C

I nev - er let them down. ___
you're burn-in' me a - live. ___

G C F C

When it comes to love I keep my sen - ses,
I can't de - ny you e-ven when I catch you,

G C F C

I don't get kicked a - round. ___
weav-in' a weak al - i - bi. ___

Fm/C

(1., D.S.) I shiv-ered once _ you broke in - to my soul. _
'Cause when the night falls, you make me for - get, _

C D

___ The dam-age is done _ now, I'm out of con - trol. ___
___ your love is kill-ing me, and it ain't o - ver yet.

To Coda

N.C. G C

How did you get to me? No One Else On Earth

Copyright © 1989 Sony Tunes Inc., Chalk Hill Music, Sony Tree Publishing Co., Inc.,
Edisto Sound International, EMI Golden Torch Music Corp. and Heart Street Music
All Rights on behalf of Sony Tunes Inc., Chalk Hill Music, Sony Tree Publishing Co., Inc. and Edisto Sound
International Administered by Sony Music Publishing, 8 Music Square West, Nashville, TN 37203
All Rights for Heart Street Music Controlled and Administered by EMI Golden Torch Music Corp.
International Copyright Secured All Rights Reserved

F F/C C G
could ev - er hurt me, break my heart the way you do.
C F/C C G C
No One Else On Earth
F F/C C Eb
was ev - er worth it. No one can love me like,
F 1. G Csus F F/C C
no one can love me like you.
G Csus F C 2. G C D.S. al Coda
you.
CODA
G C F F/C C
No One Else On Earth could ev - er hurt me,
G C F C
break my heart the way you do.
G C F F/C C
No One Else On Earth was ev - er worth it.
Eb F Repeat and Fade
No one can love me like, no one can hurt me like,

OKIE FROM MUSKOGEE

Words and Music by MERLE HAGGARD
and ROY EDWARD BURRIS

Moderately fast

Eb

We don't smoke mar-i - jua-na in Mus - ko - gee, ___
We don't make a par-ty out of lov - ing, ___
boots are still in style if a man needs foot-wear, ___

And we don't take our trips on L. S.
But we like hold - ing hands and pitch-ing
Beads and Ro - man san - dals won't be

Bb7

D. And we don't burn our
woo. We don't let our
seen. Foot - balls' still the

draft cards down on Main Street, But
hair grow long and shag - gy Like the
rough - est thing on cam - pus, And the

Eb

we like liv - ing right and be - ing free. ___
hip - pies out in San Fran - cis - co do. ___
kids here still re - spect the Col - lege Dean. ___

Copyright © 1969 Sony Tree Publishing Co., Inc.
This arrangement Copyright © 1995 Sony Tree Publishing Co., Inc.
All Rights Administered by Sony Music Publishing, 8 Music Square West, Nashville, TN 37203
International Copyright Secured All Rights Reserved

And I'm proud to be an O-kie From Mus-
ko-gee; A place where e-ven
Bb7
squares can have a ball.
We still wave Ol' Glo-ry down at the
Court House, White
light-ning's still the big-gest thrill of all.
Eb
1.,2.
3.
(3.) Leath-er

ON THE OTHER HAND

Words and Music by DON SCHLITZ
and PAUL OVERSTREET

Easy Country Swing (♫-♩♪)

F F7

On one hand, I count the rea - sons I could
arms I feel the pas - sion I

B♭ F

stay with you, and hold you close to
thought had died. When I looked in - to your

C7 F

me all night long So man-y lov-ers'
eyes I found my-self. When I first kissed your

F7 B♭

games I'd love to play with you on that
lips I felt so a-live. I've got to

G7 C7

hand there's no rea-son why it's wrong.
hand it to you girl you're some-thing else.

© Copyright 1985 by MCA MUSIC PUBLISHING, A Division of MCA INC.,
DON SCHLITZ MUSIC, SCREEN GEMS-EMI MUSIC INC. and SCARLET MOON MUSIC
All Rights for DON SCHLITZ MUSIC Controlled and Administered by MCA MUSIC
PUBLISHING, A Division of MCA INC.
International Copyright Secured All Rights Reserved
MCA music publishing

N.C.
B♭
But On The Oth-er Hand, there's a
F
C7
gold-en hand to re-mind me of some-
F
one who would not un-der-stand On
B♭
F
one hand I could stay and be your lov-ing man,
C7
but the rea-son I must go is On The
F
1.
Oth-er Hand.
2.
C7
In your Yeah, the rea-son I must
F
go is On The Oth-er Hand.

PICKUP MAN

Words and Music by HOWARD PERDEW
and KERRY KURT PHILLIPS

Copyright © 1994 by Modar Music (BMI), Songwriters Ink (BMI), Emdar Music (ASCAP)
and Texas Wedge Music (ASCAP)
International Copyright Secured All Rights Reserved

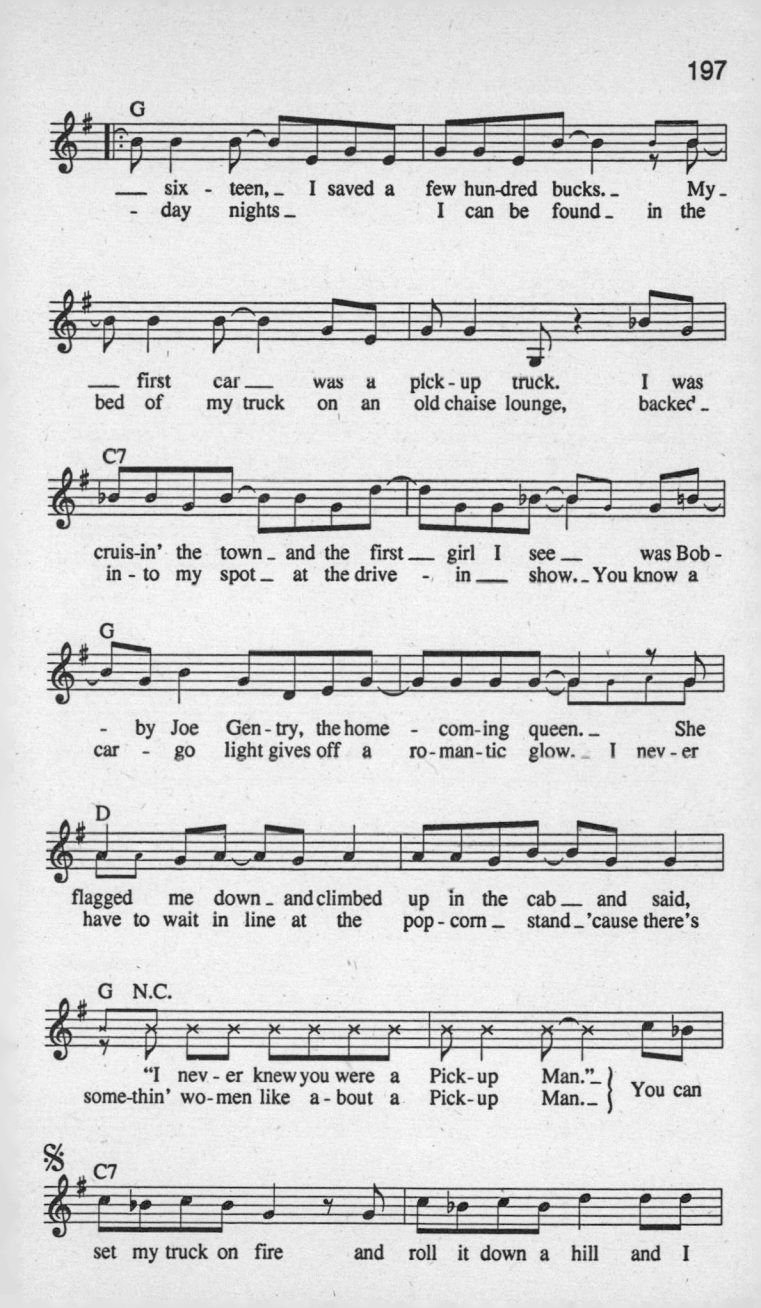
G
six - teen, I saved a few hun-dred bucks. My
- day nights I can be found in the
first car was a pick-up truck. I was
bed of my truck on an old chaise lounge, backed
C7
cruis-in' the town and the first girl I see was Bob -
in - to my spot at the drive - in show. You know a
G
- by Joe Gen - try, the home - com-ing queen. She
car - go light gives off a ro-man-tic glow. I nev - er
D
flagged me down and climbed up in the cab and said,
have to wait in line at the pop - corn stand 'cause there's
G N.C.
"I nev - er knew you were a Pick-up Man."
some-thin' wo-men like a-bout a Pick-up Man.
You can
C7
set my truck on fire and roll it down a hill and I

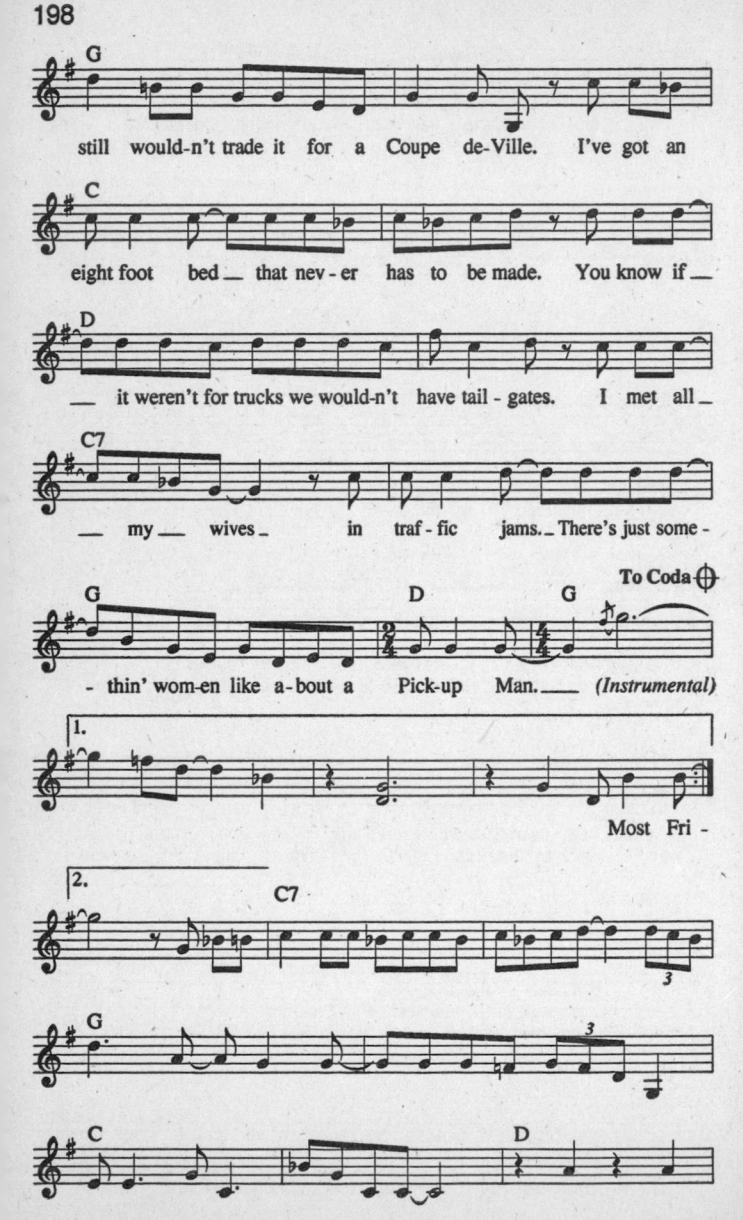
G
still would-n't trade it for a Coupe de-Ville. I've got an
C
eight foot bed that nev - er has to be made. You know if
D
it weren't for trucks we would-n't have tail - gates. I met all
C7
my wives in traf - fic jams. There's just some -
To Coda
G
D
G
- thin' wom-en like a-bout a Pick-up Man. (Instrumental)
1.
Most Fri -
2.
C7
3
G
3
C
D

C
A buck - et of rust or a
D
brand new ma - chine, once a - round the block and you'll
D.S. al Coda
know what I mean. You can
CODA
N.C.
Yeah, there's some - thin' wom-en like a - bout a
D
G
Pick-up Man.
(Instrumental)
Repeat and Fade

A RAINY NIGHT IN GEORGIA

Words and Music by
TONY JOE WHITE

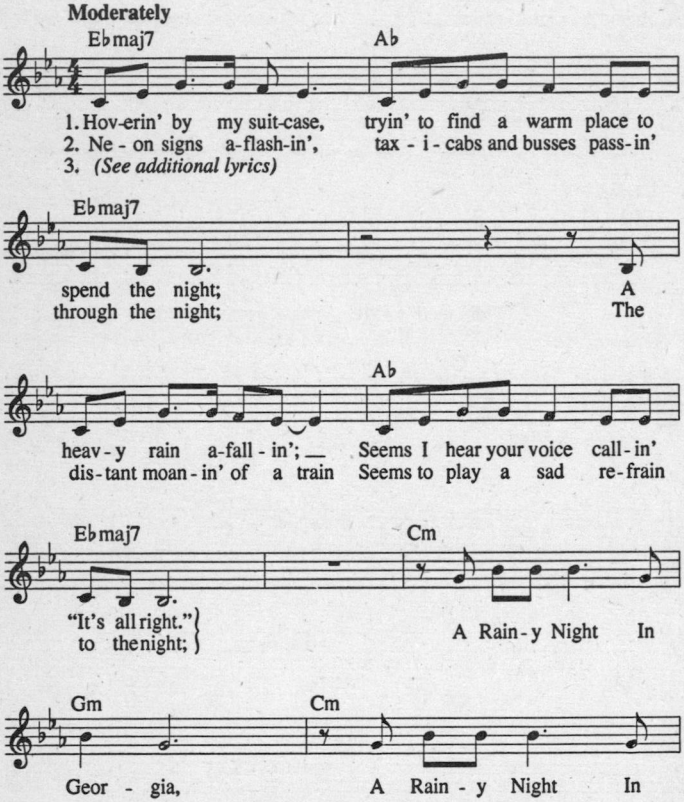

© 1969 TEMI COMBINE INC.
All Rights Controlled by COMBINE MUSIC CORP. and Administered by EMI BLACKWOOD MUSIC INC.
All Rights Reserved International Copyright Secured Used by Permission

Additional Lyrics

3. I find me a place in a box car,
So I take out my guitar to pass some time;
Late at night when it's hard to rest,
I hold your picture to my chest, and I'm all right;
Chorus

ROCKY TOP

Words and Music by BOUDLEAUX BRYANT
and FELICE BRYANT

Copyright © 1967 by HOUSE OF BRYANT PUBLICATIONS, Gatlinburg, TN
This arrangement Copyright © 1995 by HOUSE OF BRYANT PUBLICATIONS, Gatlinburg, TN
International Copyright Secured All Rights Reserved

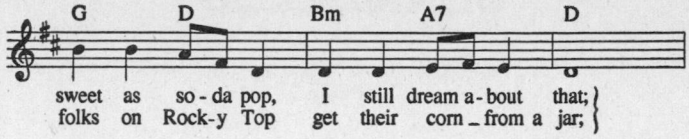

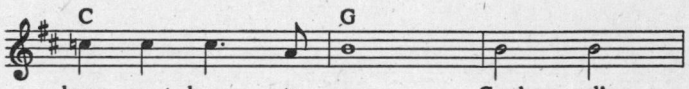

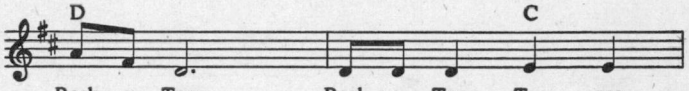

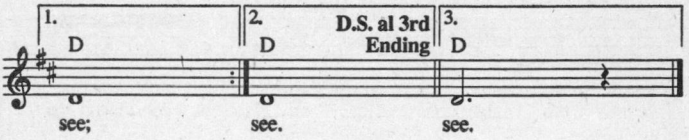

Additional Lyrics

3. I've had years of cramped-up city life
Trapped like a duck in a pen;
All I know is it's a pity life
Can't be simple again.
Chorus

SHAMELESS

Words and Music by
BILLY JOEL

© 1988 JOEL SONGS
All Rights Controlled and Administered by EMI BLACKWOOD MUSIC INC.
All Rights Reserved International Copyright Secured Used by Permission

to fall. You know
you please. You see in

I'm not a man who's ev - er been in - se -
all my life I've nev - er found what I

cure a - bout the world I've been liv - ing in. I
could-n't re - sist, what I could-n't turn down. I could

don't break eas - y. I have my pride. But if
walk a-way from an - y - one I ev - er knew but I

you need to be sat - is - fied I'm can't walk a - way from

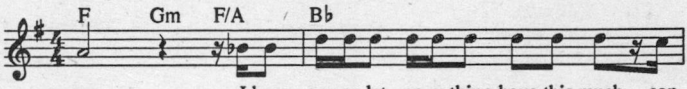

you. I have nev-er let an-y-thing have this much con-

trol o-ver me. I worked too hard to call my life my

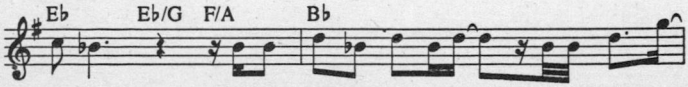

own. Well, I made my-self a world and it worked so

Am
Ab
per-fect-ly.
But it's your world now. I can't re-fuse.
Am
D7
I nev-er had so much to lose.
I'm
G
D/F#
Shame-less.
(Instrumental)
Em
C
Bb/C
G
D/F#
Em
C
C/Bb
Em
Em/D
C
Bb/C
You know it
D
B/D#
should be eas - y for a man who's strong
to
Em
Am7
say he's sor - ry or ad - mit where he's wrong
I've

D
B/D#
nev - er lost an - y - thing I ev - er missed but
Em
F
I've nev - er been in love like this.
It's out of my hands. I'm
G
Shame - less.
Shame - less.
I don't have the
(Vocal ad lib.)
D/F#
pow - er now.
But I don't want it
Em
an - y - how.
So I've got to let it
C
B♭/C
G
go.
I'm Shame-less,
Shame-less as a
D/F#
man can be.
You can make a to - tal
Repeat and Fade
Em
C
B♭/C
fool of me.
I just want-ed you to know.
I'm

SHE IS HIS ONLY NEED

Words and Music by
DAVE LOGGINS

© Copyright 1992 by MCA MUSIC PUBLISHING, A Division of MCA INC. and EMERALD RIVER MUSIC
All Rights Controlled and Administered by MCA MUSIC PUBLISHING, A Division of MCA INC.
International Copyright Secured All Rights Reserved

MCA music publishing

G
C/D
He knew the way in a small ca - fe. Found.

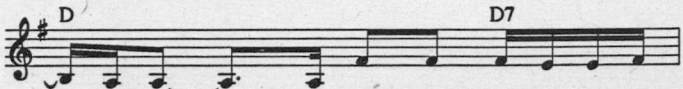
D
D7
the will: he met Miss Bon - nie and a

G
lit - tle bit of her was a lit - tle too much.

Em7
Am
G/B
A few mov - ies and a few months lat - er

Cmaj7
the feel - ing got strange e - nough.

D
He did - n't own a car so it must have been

G
Gmaj7
C
love:

D
D7
I drove him up - town for a dia

G
C/D
mond. That's when he start - ed go - in'
G
o - ver the line.
Am7
Work-ing o - ver - time
D7
to give her things just to hear her say she don't
G
C/D
de - serve 'em. But he loved her and he just kept
G
go - in' o - ver - board,
Am7
o - ver the lim - it to af - ford
D7
to give her things he knew she want - ed.

G
Gmaj7
'Cause with - out her where
Am7
would he be?
D7
See, it's not for him.
To Coda
G
C/D
G
She Is His On - ly Need.
C/D
G
Ring on her fin-ger and one on the lad-der.
Am7
A new pro-mo-tion ev-'ry now and then.
D
Bon-nie worked un-til she could-n't tie her ap-ron, then
G
C/D
stayed at home and had the first of two chil -

dren. And my, how the time ____ did fly!

The ba - bies grew up and moved _ a - way. ____

Left 'em sit - ting on the front porch rock - ing __ and

Bil - ly watch - ing Bon - nie's hair ____ turn

gray. And ev - 'ry once in a while you could

see him get up __ and he'd _ head _ down - town

'cause he'd heard a - bout some - thing she'd want - ed _

__ and it just had __ to be found. __

D
Did - n't mat - ter how sim - ple or how much. It was
G
Gmaj7
C
love.
D
D7
And boy, ain't that love just some - thing
D.S. al Coda
G
C/D
when it's strong e - nough to keep a man go - in'
CODA
G
Am7
Need.
(O - ver the line,
work-ing o - ver-time.
(Instrumental on repeat)
D7
G
C/D
His on - ly need.
She Is His On - ly Need.)
G
Am7
Just for her..
(O - ver-board,
o - ver the lim-it.
Repeat and Fade
D7
G
C/D
His on - ly need.
She Is His On - ly Need.)

SHE THINKS HIS NAME WAS JOHN

Words and Music by SANDY KNOX
and STEVE ROSEN

Copyright © 1994 Bash Music (BMI) and Mighty Nice Music (BMI)
All Rights Administered by Bluewater Music Corp.
International Copyright Secured All Rights Reserved

C/E
F
Am
G/B
put her fin - ger on. There is one who
knew that it was wrong, but too much wine and she
pit - y, what a loss." And in the end, when she was
C
G/B
Am7
C/G
nev - er leaves her thoughts And She Thinks His
left his bed at dawn. And She Thinks His
bare - ly hang - in' on, all she could say is she
1.
To Coda
F
G
C
Am
G/B
Name Was John. (Instrumental)
Name Was
thinks his name was
2.
C
G/B
F/A
C/G
F
G/B
John. (Instrumental)
D.C. al Coda
C
Dm
C/E
Fsus2
CODA
Dm7
F
John.
She
Am7
C/G
F
G
C
Thinks His Name Was John.
Am
G/B
C
(Instrumental)

SIXTEEN TONS

Words and Music by
MERLE TRAVIS

Copyright © 1947 by Unichappell Music Inc. and Elvis Presley Music
Copyright Renewed
All Rights Administered by Unichappell Music Inc.
International Copyright Secured All Rights Reserved

what do you get? An -
oth - er day old - er and
deep - er in debt. Saint
Pe - ter, don't you call me 'cause
Am
Em
I can't go I owe my soul to the
1.
com - pa - ny store.
2.
I was

SNOWBIRD

Words and Music by
GENE MacLELLAN

© 1970 BEECHWOOD MUSIC OF CANADA
All Rights for the U.S.A. and Canada Controlled and Administered by BEECHWOOD MUSIC CORP.
All Rights Reserved International Copyright Secured Used by Permission

Em
Dm
song he al - ways sings and
emp - ti - ness with - in for the
ev - er is un - true, and
with you when you go to that
G7
speaks to me of flow - ers that will
thing I want the most in life is the
if I could, you know that I would
land of gen - tle breez - es where the
1.-3.
C
bloom a - gain in spring. When
thing that I can't win.
fly a - way with you. The
peace - ful wa - ters
4.
C
G7
flow. Yeah, if I could you know
F
Dm7
that I would fly a-way with
C
you.

SOMEWHERE IN MY BROKEN HEART

Words and Music by BILLY DEAN
and RICHARD LEIGH

© 1989 EMI BLACKWOOD MUSIC INC., EMI APRIL MUSIC INC., and LION-HEARTED MUSIC
All Rights for LION-HEARTED MUSIC Controlled and Administered by EMI APRIL MUSIC INC.
All Rights Reserved International Copyright Secured Used by Permission

F
G/F
F
I, I will keep my love un - spo - ken

Em
Dm
C
3
Gsus
G
Some-where In My Bro - ken Heart.

C
Em7
Fmaj7
C/G
G
I hope that in time you will find what you long for.

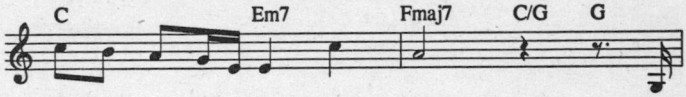
C
Em7
Fmaj7
C/G
G
Love that's writ - ten in the stars. And

To Coda
Am7
Em7
Fmaj7
Esus
E7
when you fin - 'lly do, I think you will see it's

F
C/G
G
C
D.S. al Coda
Some-where In My Bro - ken Heart.

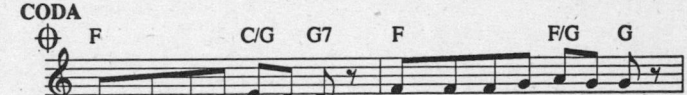
CODA
F
C/G
G7
F
F/G
G
some-where in my bro - ken, some-where in my bro - ken,

F
C/G
G
C
C/E
Some-where In My Bro - ken Heart.

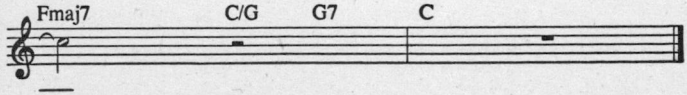
Fmaj7
C/G
G7
C

STRAIGHT TEQUILA NIGHT

Words and Music by DEBBIE HUPP
and KENT ROBBINS

Moderate Country Rock

A E

If you real - ly wan-na know she
glass of cha - blis and some

D A E

comes here a lot. She just loves to hear the mu-sic and dance.
quar - ters in change. May-be you can turn her love life a - round.

D A E

K - thir - teen is her fa -
Then she won't need the salt or the lime.

D A E

- vor-ite song. If you play it you might have a chance.
an - y - more to shoot that old mem - o - ry down.

D F#m E

To-night she's on - ly sip-ping white wine. She's
Just re-mem-ber her heart's on the mend if you

D E

friend-ly and fun - lov-ing most of the time.
ev - er come back to see her a - gain.

Copyright © 1991 Dixie Stars Music, Irving Music, Inc. and Colter Bay Music
International Copyright Secured All Rights Reserved

A E D E
But don't ask her on a Straight Te-qui - la Night.
Don't ask her on a Straight Te-qui - la Night.
A E D E
She'll start think-ing a-bout him, then she's read-y to fight.
A E D E
Blames her bro-ken heart on ev-'ry man in sight.
A E D E F#m D
on a Straight Te-qui - la Night.
E F#m D E
1.
2.
Here's a
A E D E
Don't ask her on a Straight Te-qui - la Night.
A E D E
She'll start think-ing a-bout him, then she's read-y to fight.
A E D E
Blames her bro-ken heart on ev-'ry man in sight.
Repeat and Fade
A E D E
on a Straight Te-qui - la Night.

TO ALL THE GIRLS I'VE LOVED BEFORE

Lyric by HAL DAVID
Music by ALBERT HAMMOND

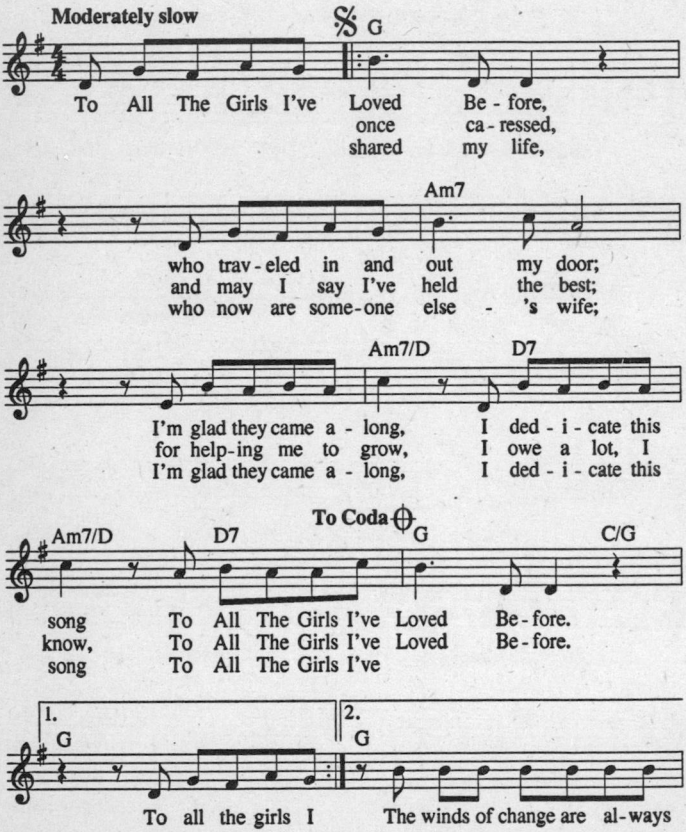

© 1975, 1984 EMI APRIL MUSIC INC. and CASA DAVID
All Rights Reserved International Copyright Secured Used by Permission

C/G G
blow - ing and ev - 'ry - time I tried to
Am7 Am7/D
stay. The winds of change con - tin - ued
D7 Am7/D D7
blow - ing, and they just car - ried me a -
D.S. al Coda
G C/G G
way. To all the girls who
CODA
C/G G Eb7sus
Loved Be-fore. To all the girls who
Ab
cared for me, who filled my nights with
Bbm7
ec - sta - sy; they live with - in my
Bbm7/Eb Eb7 Bbm7/Eb Eb7
heart; I'll al - ways be a part of all the girls I've
Ab Db/Ab Ab
loved be - fore. The winds of change are al - ways

Db/Ab Ab
blow - ing and ev - 'ry-time I tried to
Bbm7 Bbm7/Eb
stay. The winds of change con - tin - ued
Eb7 Bbm7/Eb Eb7
blow-ing, and they just car - ried me a -
Ab
way. To all the girls we've
loved be - fore; who trav-eled in and
Bbm7
out our door; we're glad they came a -
Bbm7/Eb Eb7 Bbm7 Eb7
long; we ded - i cate this song to all the girls we've
1.
Db/Ab Ab Db/Ab Ab
loved be - fore. To all the girls we've
2.
Fb Gb Ab
loved be - fore.

WHEN SHE CRIES

Words and Music by MARC BEESON
and SONNY LeMAIRE

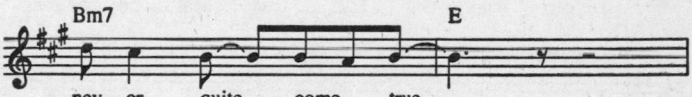

© 1992 EMI APRIL MUSIC INC. and LONGITUDE MUSIC CO.
All Rights Reserved International Copyright Secured Used by Permission

E
D/A
A
E/G#
her love kept me try - ing.
Just once I'd like to make it.
F#m7
Bm7
A/B
She does her best to hide the
Then they'll be tears of joy that
E
A
pain that she's been through.
fill her lov - ing eyes.
When She Cries.
A/D
A/C#
at night and she does -
D.S. (Instrumental)
Bm7
E7
D/A
A
E/F#
F#m7
- n't think that I can hear her, she tries
A/D
A/C#
to hide all the fear
F#m7/B
B7
Bm7/E
E
she feels in - side. So I pray,
A/D
A/C#
this time, I can be

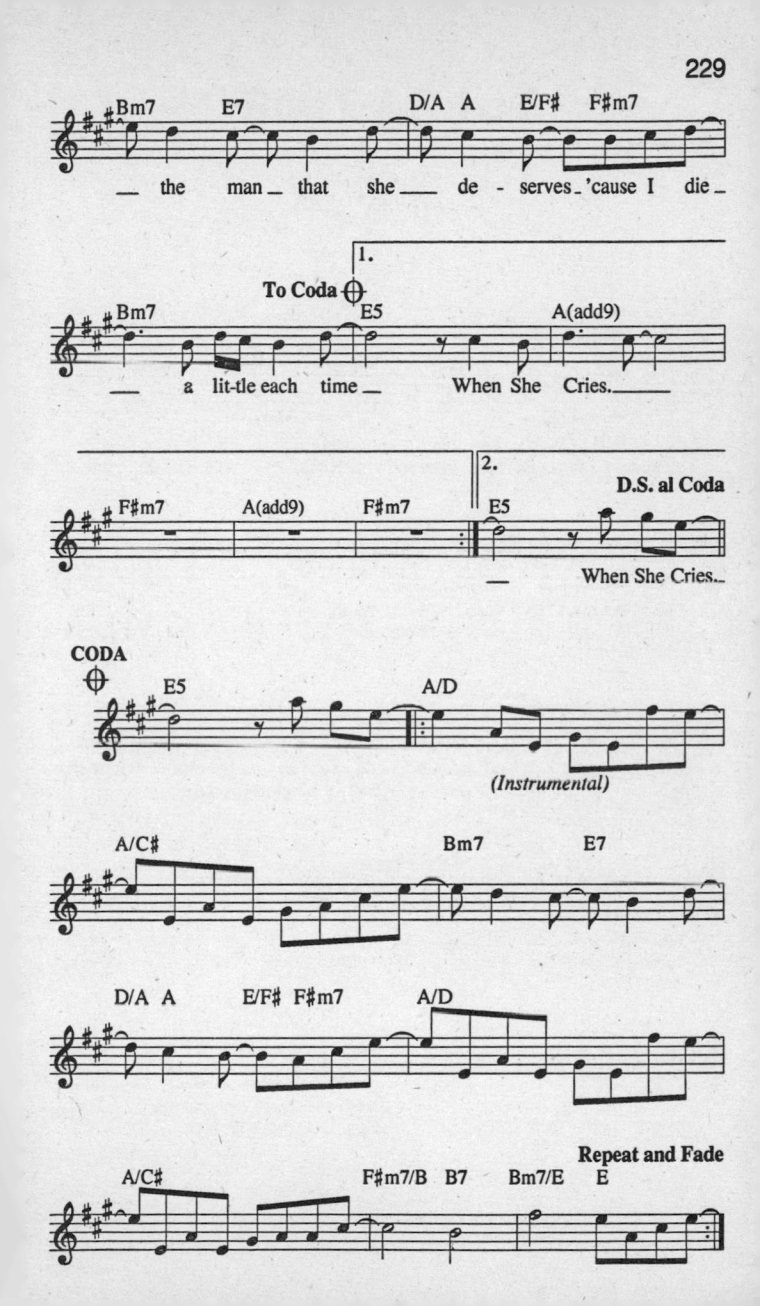
Bm7
E7
D/A A
E/F♯
F♯m7
the man that she de - serves 'cause I die
1.
To Coda
Bm7
E5
A(add9)
a lit-tle each time
When She Cries.
2.
D.S. al Coda
F♯m7
A(add9)
F♯m7
E5
When She Cries.
CODA
E5
A/D
(Instrumental)
A/C♯
Bm7
E7
D/A A
E/F♯ F♯m7
A/D
Repeat and Fade
A/C♯
F♯m7/B B7
Bm7/E E

TULSA TIME

Words and Music by
DANNY FLOWERS

Copyright © 1978 PolyGram International Publishing, Inc.
International Copyright Secured All Rights Reserved

goin' to show 'em all ___ this time, ___ 'Cause you
real - ly had a flash _ this time, ___ I

know I ain't no fool-in' I don't need no more school-in', I was
had no bus-'ness leav-in' and no - bod - y would be griev - in' if I

born to just ___ walk ___ the line. ___
went on back to Tul - sa Time. ___

Liv - in' on Tul - sa Time. ___
Liv - in' on Tul - sa Time. ___

Liv - in' on Tul - sa Time. ___ Well, you
Liv - in' on Tul - sa Time. ___ Gon - na

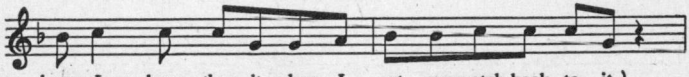

know I been thru it when I set my watch back to it,
set my watch back to it, 'cause you know I've been thru it,

liv - in' on ___ Tul - sa Time. ___ Well, ___

THE VOWS GO UNBROKEN

(Always True To You)

Words and Music by GARY BURR
and ERIC KAZ

© Copyright 1988 by MCA MUSIC PUBLISHING, A Division of MCA INC.,
GARY BURR MUSIC and ZENA MUSIC
All Rights for GARY BURR MUSIC Controlled and Administered by MCA MUSIC PUBLISHING, A Division of MCA Inc
International Copyright Secured All Rights Reserved
MCA music publishing

To Coda
D.S. al Coda
G A D G D/A A D
love keep and hon - or, al - ways true to you. Though
CODA
D Bm E/G# A D/F#
you. I knew from the first that for bet - ter or worse I'd
Bm E7 Asus A
stand by you all my life. And The
D A D G A
Vows Go Un - bro - ken. And you still know I
D D/F# G A D G
do love keep and hon - or,
D/A A D G D G
al - ways true to you. Love keep and hon - or,
D/A A D A/D G/D D A/D G/D D
al - ways true to you.

WHAT'S FOREVER FOR

Words and Music by
RAFE VAN HOY

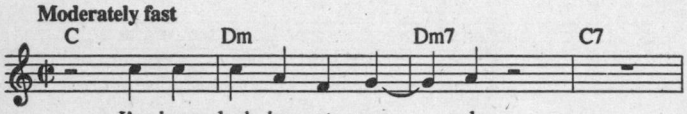

I've been look-ing at peo - ple
May-be it's me that's gone cra - zy,
I've been listen-ing to peo - ple

and how they change with the times; ___
'Cause I can't fig - ure out why; ___
and they say love is the key; ___

And late - ly all I've ___ been
all these lov - ers ___ keep
And it's not my way to let them

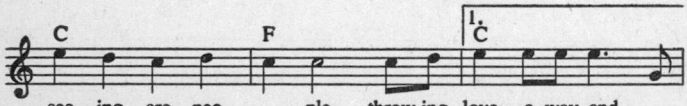

see - ing are peo - ple throw-ing love a-way and ___
hurt - ing each oth - er, when
lead me a - stray; It's

Copyright © 1978 Sony Tree Publishing Co., Inc.
This arrangement Copyright © 1995 Sony Tree Publishing Co., Inc.
All Rights Administered by Sony Music Publishing, 8 Music Square West, Nashville, TN 37203
International Copyright Secured All Rights Reserved

G7sus
G7
los - ing their minds;
2., 3.
C
Dm7
good love is so hard to come by;
on - ly that I want to be - lieve;
C
Am
So what's the glo - ry in liv -
Dm7
G7sus
G7
C
- ing? Does-n't an - y - bod - y
Dm7
G7sus
G7
ev - er stay to - geth - er an - y - more?
C
Dm7
C
And if love nev - er lasts for - ev -
Fine
Dm7
C
G
C
- er, tell me What's For-ev - er For?
F
Em7
I see love hun - gry peo - ple tryin' their best.

Am
Dm7
to sur - vive, while in their head they dream of ro -
Em7
F
G7sus
- mance, if they can keep it a - live;
G7
C
Am
Dm
So what's the glo - ry in liv -
G7sus
G7
C
- ing? Does-n't an - y - bod - y
Am
Dm7
G7sus
G7
ev - er stay to - geth - er an - y - more?
C
Dm
C
And if love nev - er lasts for - ev -
F
C
- er, tell me What's For - ev -
D.C. al Fine
G7
C
Dm7
- er For?

WILD ONE

Words and Music by WILL RAMBEAUX,
JAIME KYLE and PAT BUNCH

Copyright © 1993 Reynsong Publishing Corporation, Howe Sound Music, WB Music Corp.,
Daniel The Dog Songs, Warner-Tamerlane Publishing Corp. and Pat Bunch Publishing
International Copyright Secured All Rights Reserved

F C G C
One with an an - gel's face. She's a wom -
F C G C
- an child in a state of grace. When she was
Am Em
three years old on her dad - dy's knee, he said, "You
F
can be an - y - thing you want to be."
G F G
She's a Wild One run - nin'
1. C F C G C F
free.
(Instrumental)
G C
2. C F C G
free.
(Instrumental)
C F G C Am
She has fu - ture plans
F
and dreams at night.

Am
When they tell her life is hard, she says, "That's al - right,
G
F
C
yeah." She's a Wild One with an an -
G
C
F
C
- gel's face. She's a wom - an child in a state
G
C
Am
of grace. When she was three years old on her dad -
Em
F
- dy's knee, he said, "You can be an - y - thing
1.
G
you want to be." She's a Wild
2.
G
F
you want to be." She'a a Wild
G
C
F
One run - nin' free.
C
G
C
F
G
C
(Instrumental)

WHY ME?
(Why Me, Lord?)

Words and Music by
KRIS KRISTOFFERSON

© 1972 RESACA MUSIC PUBLISHING CO.
All Rights Controlled and Administered by EMI BLACKWOOD MUSIC INC.
All Rights Reserved International Copyright Secured Used by Permission

C
G
Lord, help me, Je - sus, I've wast - ed it
D7
so, Help me, Je - sus, I know what I
G
G7
C
am. But now that I
G
know that I've need - ed you, So, help me
1.
To Coda
D7
G
Je - sus, my soul's in your hands.
D7
3
2.
G
G7
D.S. al Coda
Try me, Lord, hands.
CODA
G
D7
hands. Je - sus, my
C
Bm
Am
G
soul's in your hands.

YOU DECORATED MY LIFE

Words and Music by DEBBIE HUPP
and BOB MORRISON

© 1978 TEMI COMBINE INC.
All Rights Controlled by MUSIC CITY MUSIC, INC. and Administered by EMI APRIL MUSIC INC.
All Rights Reserved International Copyright Secured Used by Permission

Bm/G
bod - y could see all the chang-es in me by the
a - ble to see all the things life can be shin-in'
Am/G
D
G
Gmaj9
look in my face.
soft in your eyes.
And You
C
C/D
G
C
B7
Dec-o-rat-ed My Life, cre-a-ted a
Em
Em/D
Am7
world where dream are a part.
D
G
Gmaj9
C
C/D
And You Dec-o-rat-ed My
G
C
B7
Em
Life by paint-ing your love
Em/D
Am7
D
all o-ver my heart; You Dec-o-rat-ed My
G
B7
1.
C
Life. (Instrumental)
2.
C
Gmaj9
Like a (Instrumental)

YOU DON'T KNOW ME

Words and Music by CINDY WALKER
and EDDY ARNOLD

Copyright © 1955 by Unichappell Music Inc.
Copyright Renewed
International Copyright Secured All Rights Reserved

Dm7 G7 C F C C7
ev - er been, but You Don't Know Me. For
F Cmaj7 C♯dim7
I nev - er knew the art of mak-ing love, though my
Dm G9 C Am
heart ached with love for you. A - fraid and shy, I
Em D7
let my chance go by, the chance you might have loved me
G7 C
too. You give your hand to me and then you
C7 F
say good-bye. I watch you walk a - way be-side the
F♯dim7 C A7
luck - y guy. To nev - er, nev - er know the one who
Dm7 G7 C F
loves you so; no, You Don't Know Me.
1. C G7 G7♯5
2. C
You give your

YOU LOOK SO GOOD IN LOVE

Words and Music by KERRY CHATER, RORY BOURKE and GLEN BALLARD

Copyright © 1983 SONGS OF POLYGRAM INTERNATIONAL, INC., CHAPPELL & CO.
and MCA MUSIC PUBLISHING, A Division of MCA INC.
International Copyright Secured All Rights Reserved

MCA music publishing

G Bm7 Am
So Good In Love.
D G 1. D
I wish you still want - ed me.
2. Bm Am D
(Instrumental)
G Eb7
Ab Cm7 Bbm
(Spoken:) Darling I've wasted a lot of years not seeing the real you.
So Good In Love. You
Eb Ab Eb
But tonight your beauty is shining through.
want him that's ea - sy to see. You Look
Ab Cm7 Bbm
And I never took the time to let you know.
So Good In Love.
Eb
So before he takes you away, please let
I wish you still want - ed
Ab 1. Eb 2. Eb D.S. and Fade
me say (Sung:) You Look
me. You Look

YOU NEEDED ME

Words and Music by
RANDY GOODRUM

Copyright © 1975, 1978 by Chappell & Co. and Ironside Music
This arrangement Copyright © 1995 by Chappell & Co. and Ironside Music
All Rights Administered by Chappell & Co.
International Copyright Secured All Rights Reserved

G/D B/D# Em A
high that I can al - most see e - ter - ni - ty, You
To Coda
D7 G B/D#
Need-ed Me, You Need-ed Me; and I
Em G/D C G/B
can't be-lieve it's you, I can't be - lieve it's true. I
Am7 D11 G B7
need-ed you and you were there and I'll
Em G/D
nev - er leave. Why should I leave I'd be
C G/B A7/C# A7
a fool 'cause I've fin-'lly found some-one who real - ly cares.
D.S. al Coda
D7sus D7
You held my
CODA
G E7
Need-ed Me, You
A7 D7 G
Need-ed Me, You Need-ed Me.

YOUR CHEATIN' HEART

Words and Music by
HANK WILLIAMS

Copyright © 1952 by Hiriam Music and Acuff-Rose Music, Inc. in the U.S.A.
Copyright Renewed
All Rights for Hiriam Music Administered by Rightsong Music Inc.
All Rights outside the U.S.A. Controlled by Acuff-Rose Music, Inc.
International Copyright Secured All Rights Reserved

C
C7
F
you When tears come down
C
like fall - in' rain You'll toss a -
D7
G7
round and call my name
C
C7
You'll walk the floor the way I
F
do Your Cheat - in'
G7
1.
C
Heart will tell on you.
G7
2.
C
Your Cheat - in' you.

GUITAR CHORD FRAMES

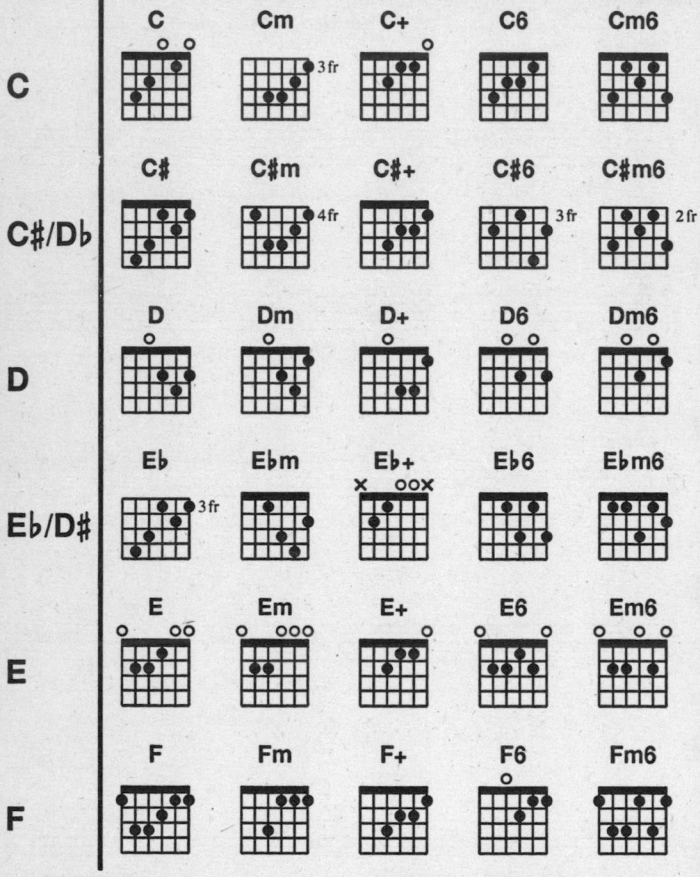

This guitar chord reference includes 120 commonly used chords. For a more complete guide to guitar chords, see "THE PAPERBACK CHORD BOOK" (HL00702009).

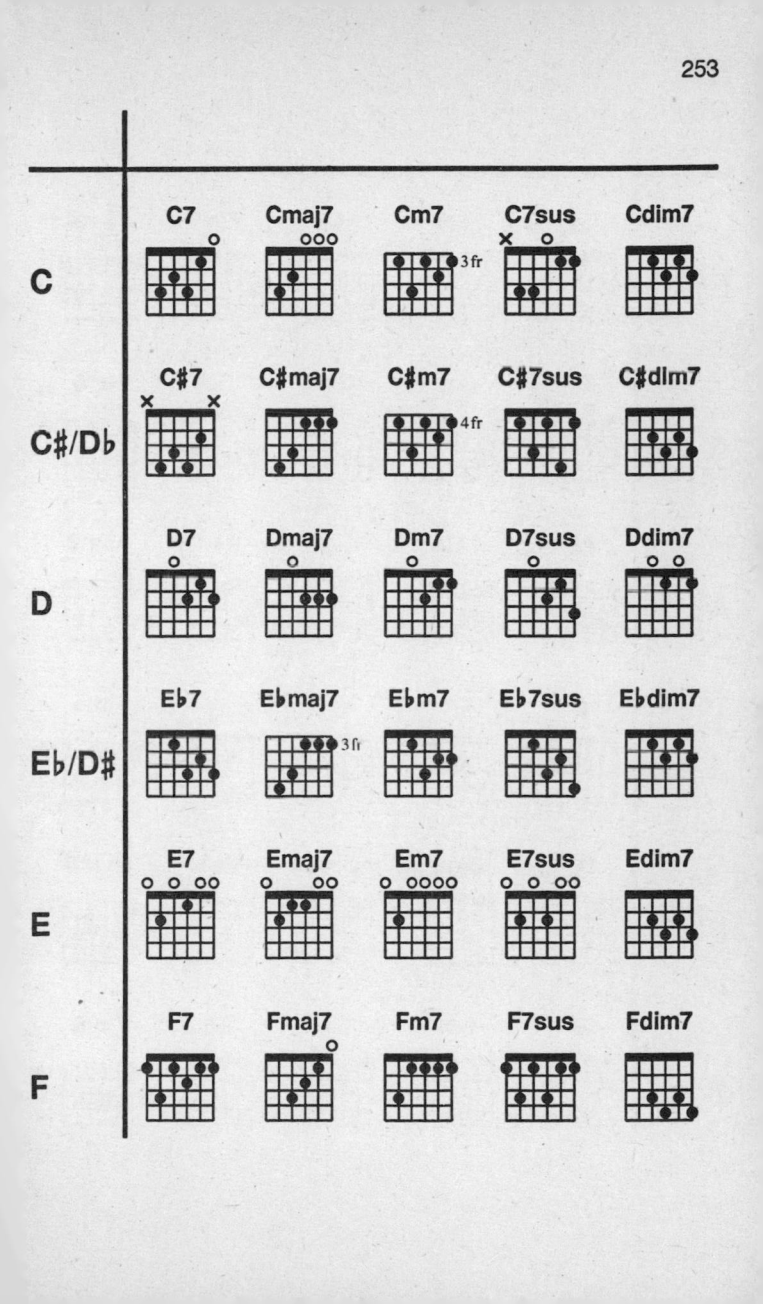
C
C7
Cmaj7
Cm7
3 fr
C7sus
Cdim7
C♯/D♭
C♯7
C♯maj7
C♯m7
4 fr
C♯7sus
C♯dim7
D
D7
Dmaj7
Dm7
D7sus
Ddim7
E♭/D♯
E♭7
E♭maj7
3 fr
E♭m7
E♭7sus
E♭dim7
E
E7
Emaj7
Em7
E7sus
Edim7
F
F7
Fmaj7
Fm7
F7sus
Fdim7

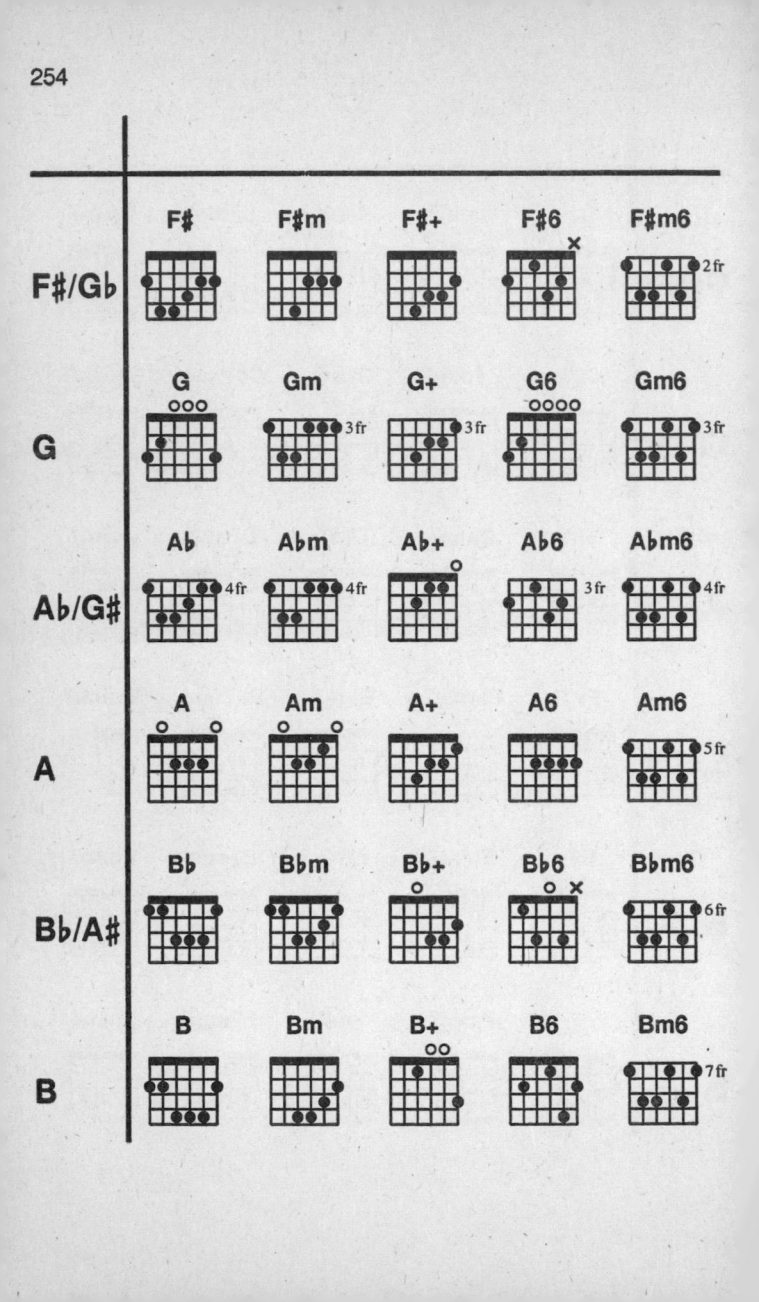
F♯/G♭
F♯
F♯m
F♯+
F♯6
F♯m6
2fr
G
G
Gm
3fr
G+
3fr
G6
Gm6
3fr
A♭/G♯
A♭
A♭m
4fr
A♭+
A♭6
3fr
A♭m6
4fr
A
A
Am
A+
A6
Am6
5fr
B♭/A♯
B♭
B♭m
B♭+
B♭6
B♭m6
6fr
B
B
Bm
B+
B6
Bm6
7fr

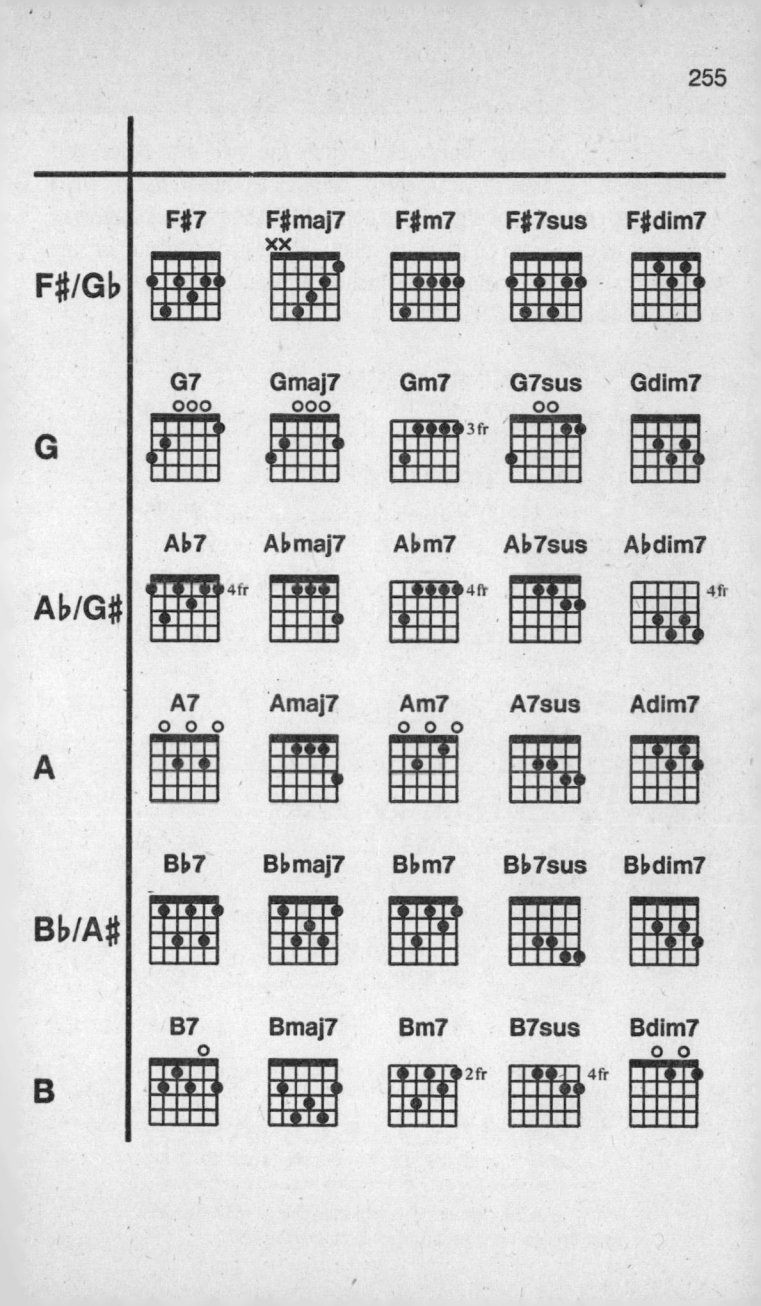
F♯/G♭
F♯7
F♯maj7
xx
F♯m7
F♯7sus
F♯dim7
G
G7
ooo
Gmaj7
ooo
Gm7
3fr
G7sus
oo
Gdim7
A♭/G♯
A♭7
4fr
A♭maj7
A♭m7
4fr
A♭7sus
A♭dim7
4fr
A
A7
o o o
Amaj7
Am7
o o o
A7sus
Adim7
B♭/A♯
B♭7
B♭maj7
B♭m7
B♭7sus
B♭dim7
B
B7
o
Bmaj7
Bm7
2fr
B7sus
4fr
Bdim7
o o

THE PAPERBACK SONGS SERIES

EAU CLAIRE DISTRICT LIBRARY

These perfectly portable paperbacks include the melodies, lyrics, and chords symbols for your favorite songs, all in a convenient, pocket-sized book. Using concise, one-line music notation, anyone from hobbyists to professionals can strum on the guitar, play melodies on the piano, or sing the lyrics to great songs. Books also include a helpful guitar chord chart. A fantastic deal - only $5.95 each!

THE BEATLES
00702008 ..... $5.95

THE BLUES
00702014 ..... $5.95

CHORDS FOR KEYBOARD & GUITAR
00702009 ..... $5.95

CLASSIC ROCK
00310058 ..... $5.95

COUNTRY HITS
00702013 ..... $5.95

THE ROCK & ROLL COLLECTION
00702020 ..... $5.95

FOR MORE INFORMATION, SEE YOUR LOCAL MUSIC DEALER, OR WRITE TO:

HAL•LEONARD™ CORPORATION

7777 W. BLUEMOUND RD. P.O. BOX 13819 MILWAUKEE, WI 53213

Prices, availability and contents subject to change without notice. Some products may not be available outside the U.S.A.

1095